THE AMERICAN

RAILROAD NETWORK

1861—1890

The American

Railroad Network

1861 — 1890

GEORGE ROGERS TAYLOR

IRENE D. NEU

Introduction by Mark Reutter

UNIVERSITY OF ILLINOIS PRESS
Urbana and Chicago

First Illinois paperback, 2003
Reprinted by arrangement with Harvard University Press
Manufactured in the United States of America

P 5 4 3 2

∞ This book is printed on acid-free paper.

Library of Congress Cataloging-in-Publication Data
Taylor, George Rogers
The American railroad network, 1861–1890 / George Rogers Taylor and
Irene D. Neu ; introduction by Mark Reutter.
p. cm.
Originally published: Cambridge, Mass. : Harvard University Press, 1956.
Includes bibliographical references and index.
ISBN 0-252-07114-x (pbk. : alk. paper)
1. Railroads—United States—History.
2. Railroad gauges—United States—History.
I. Neu, Irene D. II. Title.
HE2751.T28   2003
385'.0973'09034—DC21   2002072536

CONTENTS

CONTENTS

MAPS

(at end of book)

PREFACE

This volume grew out of the realization that the railroad maps available for the pre-Civil War years present a seriously misleading picture of the degree of physical integration of American railroads. The first task attempted was to construct a more meaningful map. When this was accomplished questions immediately arose: Why the lack of integration of the American railroad net as late as 1861? When, by what means, and why did a unified network emerge in the following three decades? Obviously a thoroughgoing answer to these questions would involve telling the whole story of American economic and transportation history in the nineteenth century — an intention far beyond the limits of this study. We have, therefore, contented ourselves with describing and emphasizing certain significant aspects of the situation and suggesting some solutions to the problems raised.

The first five chapters of this book are primarily the work of George Rogers Taylor, the last four of Irene D. Neu. But the project has been a coöperative one and the authors take joint responsibility for what is presented. The research on the first five chapters and the drafting of the maps were made possible by a grant from the Joseph B. Eastman Foundation at Amherst College. Work on the last four chapters was generously financed by the Committee on Research in Economic History. Many persons assisted the authors in one way or another. At the risk of being invidious, a few bows must be made. Arthur H. Cole from the beginning gave generously of his time and indispensably of encouragement and advice. For aid in clearing up difficult points or in going far beyond the call of duty in answering letters of enquiry we are under special obligation to: Robert C. Black, III, C. K. Brown, C. J. Corliss, Elizabeth O. Cullen, Charles E. Fisher, G. P. deT. Glazebrook, William K. Lamb, Paul F. Laning, Walter R. Marvin, Andrew Forest Muir, Richard C. Overton, Robert M. Sutton, Charles W. Turner, and D. W. Yungmeyer. For many hours of assistance in preparing the maps we are indebted to John V. Bowmer and Mary Alice Kallet.

G. R. T.
I. D. N.

INTRODUCTION TO
THE ILLINOIS PAPERBACK

Mark Reutter

Railroads were to the second half of the nineteenth century what the computer and telecommunications industries were to the final quarter of the twentieth—the drivers of economic change. Railroads provided the linkages that allowed the Industrial Revolution to gain traction. Today we take this kind of integrated networking for granted, but a century and a half ago America's transportation was anything but coordinated. "Breaking bulk" was standard practice, requiring everything from whiskey to wheat to be unloaded and transshipped along a ragged chain of wagons, carts, railroads, steamboats, and canal packets. Passengers faced the same wearisome blockages, adding to the cost, inconvenience, and slowness of getting anywhere.

Few people grasped the revolutionary possibilities of the railroad at first. The new form of transportation, invented in England in the 1820s, had two important components: it replaced animal power with mechanical power (the steam locomotive) and it directed that power upon a smooth and fixed right-of-way (a road of rails). Besides reducing trip times, the railroad permitted a regularity and ease of interchange for the long-distance movement of cars. This technology was more or less in place when the first American lines opened in the 1830s, but the psychology wasn't. Most early promoters looked upon the railroad as a feeder to waterways or a means of serving the needs of a local community. The pioneer Mohawk and Hudson Railroad ran only seventeen miles and was built to help travelers on the Erie Canal around an especially tortuous section of locks and bends. Philadelphia's first railroad was even shorter—six miles—and was aimed at providing transport for farmers and cows.

Many of the first railroads were built to accommodate English-built locomotives. This called for the inside edges of the rails to be spaced 4 feet 8½ inches apart, a width commonly used on English wagon roads and coal tramways. But a movement soon developed for alternate gauges, encouraged by merchant groups protective of their own interests. The Atlantic and St. Lawrence Railroad, running west from Portland, Maine, intentionally used a gauge of 5 feet 6 inches to build up its trade with New Hampshire and Canada, while denying business to Boston, where railroads used the gauge of 4 feet 8½ inches. The New York promoters of the Erie Railroad opted for a gauge of 6 feet to thwart rival merchants in Pennsylvania. Most railroads south of Richmond, Virginia, were built to a gauge of 5 feet, which was 3½ inches wider than the Baltimore and Ohio gauge in Maryland. Thus did a few inches divide North and South and prevent the through shipment of passengers, freight, and mail.

The question of gauges went to the heart of the debate over whether the United States would become a nation envisioned by Alexander Hamilton or one advocated by Thomas Jefferson, a land of urban factories or of self-sufficient rural farms. As the railways proved their superiority over canals and rivers and expanded over longer distances, they became carriers of the controversy. Railroads were capital intensive and needed to generate business to recoup all they could in returns as quickly as possible. They could earn the most in a rail net that became more valuable to users the more it was used by others. A standardized gauge fit a business model that placed a premium on high volume and low cost, the very principles that Hamilton had advocated for his factory system.

Yet standardization threatened the Jeffersonian world from which the railroads had sprung. The merchants and farmers who had subscribed to local railroad stocks, not to mention the hotel keepers and wagoners who made their living from the transfer of freight and passengers where lines "broke," had much to lose if trains could pass through their communities without changing cars or stations. While technical journals generally advocated a uniform gauge, politicians were more comfortable with small, fragmented railroads, and "gauge wars" sometimes erupted when railroad managements tried to make direct connections between lines.

Against this backdrop *The American Railroad Network* begins. George Rogers Taylor and Irene D. Neu stake their claim for originality in the first chapter by discounting the importance of one of the set pieces of conventional railroad history—the momentous impact of the Civil War on the industry. While the railroads influenced the course of the war, the war only reinforced "a movement which was gathering momentum in any case," according to the authors. Larger economic forces were at work, including the combination of short lines into larger systems in the 1850s; the growth of finance capitalism in New York and Boston, which replaced local control of railroad stock; and the colonization of the Midwest, where cash crops turned farming from subsistence to a money economy dependent on access to distant markets. In concert, these factors transformed the railroads from a maze of provincial pikes to remarkably unified purveyors of mass transportation.

The book provides a coherent framework for thinking about the larger business environment in which the industry exerted its influence on invention, manufacturing, and agriculture. As rail managements struggled for ways to bridge the differences in gauges after 1865, trains got longer, heavier, and faster. Rates dropped and demand increased. Rising demand required stronger materials and better appliances, creating brand new industries. Steel is a case in point. The first commercial steel rail, replacing brittle iron rail, was rolled in 1867 for the Pennsylvania Railroad. A year later, George Westinghouse sold his first set of air brakes.

Better connections between rail lines required block signaling, replacing crude semaphores and "high balls," and better scheduling advanced the science of telegraphy. Mass transportation made mass production possible, guaranteeing a regular flow of raw materials to new factories and opening up national markets for the sale of manufactured goods. Three decades of hyper-growth turned America into the world's leading industrial producer by 1890, a far cry from its second-tier status in 1860.

Taylor and Neu underscore another point that is often lost in conventional accounts of railroading; namely, that technological change is a political process. The eventual triumph of a uniform national gauge in the 1890s was not preordained but was made possible by the rules and voluntary agreements negotiated earlier by teams of managers and technical groups. It will certainly come as a surprise to many readers to learn how middle-level railroaders worked together to iron out kinks in the network and develop procedures that improved service while often reducing rates. Examining the process of railroad integration, Taylor and Neu suggest that the spectacular maneuvers of people like Jay Gould and William Vanderbilt had less impact on the day-to-day development of the business than did the technical meetings of the American Master Mechanics' Association and the through bills of lading established by fast freight lines. Cooperation proved more profitable than warfare.

When *The American Railroad Network* was published in 1956, railroad studies were generally short on analysis and long on operational details, accounts of pitched political or labor battles, and biographies of flamboyant corporate leaders. Taylor and Neu, who had been examining transportation for some time from their academic perches at Amherst College and Southeast Missouri State College, respectively, moved away from the study of moguls and scandals to concentrate on the meaning of railroads as a whole. Since then, scholars have gained a greater understanding of the underlying trends of technology, finance, and bureaucratic organization whose effects were so strikingly illustrated in the rise of the railroads. It is a tribute to the book's influence that a number of subsequent works have traced more thoroughly the phenomena outlined on the pages that follow. Long out of print, this study deserves to be reissued, not just for its brisk analysis of the post–Civil War "take-off" of the railroads, but also for the three superb maps that provide a freeze-frame of the business in 1861.

In addition to the obvious analogy between the growth of the integrated rail system and the networking effects of today's global information technologies, there are some parallels to be drawn between transportation past and present. On the one hand, great strides have been made in the shipment of consumer goods in standardized metal containers. Several hundred VCRs can be sealed in a "box" in Malaysia and go anywhere in North America via container ships, intermodal trains, and flatbed trucks. The penetration of low-cost freight transport into remote and formerly isolated regions has done much to make the global economy possible. Much less impressive is our domestic patchwork of passenger transportation that results in daily choke points and carnage on the highways coupled with the threadbare use of scattered and slow passenger trains. High-speed trains have proved successful in Europe and Asia, but their development has stalled in the United States. This would astound the railroad standardizers of a century ago who were willing to put progress ahead of narrow political and business interests.

Some Suggested Readings

There are a number of books about nineteenth-century railroads that stand out as integrative studies with the same broad-gauge approach of *The American Railroad Network.* A good place to start is John F. Stover's overview, *American Railroads* (University of Chicago Press, 1961; revised, 1979), and George Rogers Taylor's prelude to the railroad era, *The Transportation Revolution, 1815–1860* (Holt, Rinehart, 1951).

W. W. Rostow's *The Stages of Economic Growth* (Cambridge University Press, 1960) credits railroads for the "take-off" of the U.S. economy. Taking his cue from Taylor and Neu, Rostow notes that while "an incomplete railway line is of limited use," the post–Civil War development of "the great American continental railway networks" mobilized capital and enlarged the flow of commerce. In *The Railroads: The Nation's First Big Business* (Harcourt, Brace, 1965), Alfred D. Chandler Jr. argues that the industry did more than that. Not only did the railroads usher in the age of industry, they also invented the modern model of corporate capitalism. Railroads are at the heart of Chandler's influential treatise on management and organizational growth, *The Visible Hand: The Managerial Revolution in American Business* (Belknap Press, 1977), as well as Olivier Zunz's *Making America Corporate* (University of Chicago Press, 1990), which analyzed the personnel records of the Chicago, Burlington and Quincy Railroad in the 1880s. Robert W. Fogel's 1964 volume, *Railroads and American Economic Growth,* which used econometric models to argue that railroads were not nearly as indispensable to the nineteenth-century economy as generally believed, has been largely discredited.

The problems of controlling the big business of railroads have been examined by polemists and scholars alike. Among the books that have stood the test of time are Charles Francis Adams Jr.'s *Railroads: Their Origin and Problems* (G. P. Putnam, 1878; reissued 1981); Arthur T. Hadley's *Railroad Transportation: Its History and Its Laws* (G. P. Putnam, 1886); George H. Miller's *Railroads and the Granger Laws* (University of Wisconsin Press, 1971); Gabriel Kolko's *Railroads and Regulation* (Princeton University Press, 1965); and Albro Martin's *Enterprise Denied: Origins of the Decline of American Railroads* (Columbia University Press, 1971). Each book offers careful accounts of the complex social, political, and regulatory ramifications of the railway boom. Together these studies serve as correctives to the oversimplified "robber-baron" literature of the Progressive Era that still distorts public perceptions of the industry.

Of the flood of books specializing in the nuts and bolts of railroading, three works rise up as indispensable to the understanding of the evolution of the rail network: George W. Hilton's *American Narrow Gauge Railroads* (Stanford University Press, 1990) and John H. White Jr.'s two companion volumes, *The American Railroad Passenger Car* and *The American Railroad Freight Car* (Johns Hopkins University Press, 1978 and 1993, respectively). By conveying the issues of tracks and cars, construction and operation, faced by nineteenth-century railroad builders, Hilton and White add detail and depth to Taylor and Neu's synthesis.

THE AMERICAN RAILROAD NETWORK
1861-1890

FOCUSING THE PROBLEM

HISTORICAL BACKGROUND

The American economy, already expanding rapidly before the Civil War, continued growing with almost explosive force during the following decades. In 1860 the United States was a secondary industrial nation among the nations of the world. Before the end of the century it had achieved a position of preëminence. Its pig iron production just prior to the war was only a small fraction of that of Great Britain, and steelmaking had hardly begun. Before the end of the century the American output of both products exceeded that of any other country. It has been estimated that in 1860 the value of manufactured goods in each of the three leading countries, the United Kingdom, France, and Germany, was greater than in the United States. By 1890 the United States had not only moved into first place, but the value of its manufactures nearly equaled the combined output of the three former leaders.[1]

Fundamental improvements in railroad transportation were among the major factors making possible the post–Civil War expansion. This study focuses on only one aspect of those improvements — the conversion of the fragmented and non-unified railroads of 1860 into the relatively integrated network of three decades later — but there were, of course, other developments which greatly increased the efficiency of railroad transportation. Technological improvements in rails, roadbed, motive power, and rolling stock came in rapid succession. Steel rails, first used in this country during the Civil War, replaced the much less satisfactory iron ones. Stronger rails, roadbed, and bridges made possible the use of heavier engines and cars. In 1860 locomotives seldom weighed more than about 30 tons whereas by 1890 they might weigh as much as 85 tons. Standard capacity for freight cars, about 10 tons in 1860, had doubled by the early eighties, while a few cars of even greater capacity were already in use. A host of other developments facilitated railroad operations: the automatic coupler, the air brake, improved terminal facilities, increased use of the telegraph, and the adoption of the block system for controlling traffic. Freight locomotives on the Pennsylvania Railroad hauled on the average 2,100,000 ton miles of freight in 1870, but were handling 5,100,000 such units per annum eleven years later.[2]

This was the period of most rapid construction of new track. In 1860 there were 30,626 miles of railway in operation in the United States and 2,065 miles in Canada. The total for the two countries combined grew to about 175,000 in 1890. Before the war only one railroad had reached the Missouri River. During the following three decades transcontinental lines were completed in both the United States and Canada, and a great network had been constructed not only in the Mississippi Valley west of the river, but also in Texas, in the Mountain States, and on the Pacific coast. Even in the older area east of the Mississippi and the Great Lakes, track mileage continued to grow as gaps were filled in, bridges built, and roads constructed parallel to existing ones.

This was the period also when smaller companies were consolidated into extensive railroad systems, and when such men as Cornelius Vanderbilt, Jay Gould, and Collis P. Huntington were building their great railroad empires. Cutthroat competition put heavy pressure on railroad rates, especially in trunk-line territory. In 1858 the rate for shipping wheat by rail from Chicago to New York was 38.61 cents a bushel; in 1870 it had fallen to 26.11 cents; and in 1890 to 14.3. The average rate per ton mile charged by United States railroads just after the Civil War was 1.925 cents. This had fallen to .941 in 1890.[3] But the decline was far from uniform, for rates tended to remain relatively high where there was little competition from other rail lines or from waterways. Where parallel roads competed for traffic, as between Chicago and New York, rates were at times kept up by interline agreements. When these broke down, charges fell drastically, sometimes well below operating costs. Railroad competition proved a crushing blow to most inland water routes. Though traffic continued to grow on the Great Lakes and the Sault Canal, the weaker canals had succumbed to railroad competition during the forties and fifties. Before the eighties were over, the tonnage carried had reached its high point even on such major water routes as the Mississippi River and the Erie Canal.

Tremendous popular enthusiasm for the railroads led to grants of millions of acres of public land and extensive financial aid by federal, state, and local governments. But following the Civil War, and especially after 1873, public opinion gradually turned against the railroads. Stock watering, secret rebates, pooling agreements, political bribery, scandals like the Credit Mobilier exposé, and the public-be-damned attitude of railroad magnates gave rise to anti-railroad agitation by farmers, merchants, and investor groups. Criticism of the railroads took political form in the Granger and Anti-Monopoly movements. Efforts at state regulation were followed in 1887 by the adoption of the federal Interstate Commerce Commission Act.

The very importance of the railroad in the development of the American economy has tended to obscure the fact that it was itself affected at every stage by the economic environment in which it grew. While no general survey of these environmental factors will be attempted, this study does seek to identify the influences which were active first in erecting and then in removing barriers to the creation of a physically integrated system of national railroad transportation. First, the condition of the uncoördinated railroad net of 1861 will be examined; then, some of the important steps by which during the following three decades it evolved into a truly integrated work will be traced.

THE DOMINANCE OF LOCAL INTERESTS TO 1861

During the nineteenth century there took place in this country a gradual transition from merchant to industrial and finance capitalism. This was a development which profoundly altered the practices and the outlook of the business community. On the one hand the railroads helped to effect this change; on the other their growth was significantly affected by it.

While the merchant-dominated capitalism of the eighteenth century was a decaying institution during the early decades of the following century, the parochial viewpoint which it engendered in the business leaders of the day toward transportation development prevailed until about the time of the Civil War. While merchants ruled the American economy they constituted a business and social elite. From their counting houses

3

they organized and directed the exchange of goods and services in both domestic and foreign trade. Largely unspecialized in function, they brought together and arranged into an effective pattern the threads of an increasingly complex exchange economy. The great merchants not only bought and sold goods in large and small quantities on their own account or for others in the capacity of brokers, factors, or agents, but also performed a host of other services. They were bankers and dealers in foreign trade; they owned ships, docks, and warehouses; they bought and sold marine insurance; they held title to and sometimes operated fishing, mining, or manufacturing ventures; and they became the chief real-estate owners and speculators of their day.

The prosperity of the merchant depended in large part upon the volume of the commerce in his home port and upon the trade carried by his ships and distributed from his own warehouses. The leaders were located in the great ports of the Atlantic coast, which had become in the Colonial period important centers of world trade. Here the products of Europe, Africa, and the East, as well as those from the many smaller coastal towns on the Atlantic and the Gulf of Mexico, were assembled, and then in considerable part reëxported to foreign and domestic markets. This trade expanded greatly during the Napoleonic Wars, when, not infrequently, more than half the commerce of New York, Philadelphia, and Boston consisted of reëxports to foreign markets.

Following the defeat of Napoleon, the relative importance of the foreign reëxport trade declined. But coastwise commerce greatly expanded and trade with the interior grew as the frontier was pushed outward. There ensued a competitive struggle among the merchants of rival cities who were striving to capture as large a share as possible of the rapidly expanding trade of the hinterland. This intercity competition to dominate the inland trade was an important factor in the early decades of railroad development.

The first railroads in the United States were built, as were most of the early turnpikes and canals, to serve nearby and local needs. Such was the purpose of the early lines radiating from Boston. The Boston and Worcester, for instance, was designed primarily to secure for Boston the trade of the Worcester area and to divert it from the Blackstone Canal which led to Providence. The little railroads strung out along the Mohawk Valley in New York were constructed for the most part with local capital

4

to provide local transportation for nearby merchants and farmers. The early railroads of eastern Pennsylvania were financed and built largely by owners of coal lands who sought to make possible the movement of anthracite to New York and Pennsylvania markets. The 4½-mile Pontchartrain Railroad, completed in Louisiana in 1831, was designed merely to facilitate movement between New Orleans and the lake of that name.

As the possibilities of railway transportation became more clearly recognized, the roads were looked upon by the business groups in each large city chiefly as devices for forwarding their own interests. Rival groups therefore encouraged the building of lines which widened their own market areas, while they carefully avoided any development which might benefit the merchants of another city.[4] New York and Boston were competitors for the commerce of the Great Lakes and the Erie Canal, as were Troy and Albany on a smaller scale. Charleston sought to divert the cotton trade from Savannah, and Chicago and St. Louis fought for the rich commerce of the upper Mississippi.

A report of a special committee of the Select and Common Council of Philadelphia, urging that the city government invest generously in the stock of the proposed Pennsylvania Railroad, is illustrative of the competition among merchant groups in the pre-Civil War period. The committee declared, in part:

No one can shut his eyes to the fact, that the enterprise involves, for weal or for woe, the future prospects of Philadelphia. The trade of this city, already retarded by improvements on the North and the South, will be so curtailed by the Baltimore and Ohio Railroad at Pittsburg, and the completion of the railway from New York to Lake Erie, as to drain the public works, and impoverish the city and state. Labour among us will want its reward, business will stagnate, capital will desert our borders, and following this desertion of trade, the interest of the debt of the commonwealth will be unpaid! On the other hand, we have the means, by furnishing the nearest and best route to and from the West, of securing an unexampled prosperity to this city. Our *citizens* will not only be enriched, but the real estate and property of the *corporation* will be enhanced beyond the amount of the proposed subscription.[5]

THE INTEGRATION OF THE RAILROAD NET, 1861–1890

During and following the Civil War, the railroads came to be regarded less as agencies designed to serve the exclusive needs of a particular city or its immediate back country and more as a coördinated network whose primary function was to facilitate transportation. Though parochial interests lingered on and have, indeed, persisted to the present time, they came to be over-shadowed by larger, national considerations.

The Civil War itself brought a changed view of the role of the railroads. The need for through movement of troops and supplies focused attention on variations in gauge and on the lack of connections between railroads in the leading cities of both the North and the South. The exigencies of war highlighted the advantages which could be had from a standardized and inter-connected railroad system. But military requirements merely reënforced a movement which was gathering momentum in any case.

As long as population and agricultural production remained centered largely in the seaboard states, pressure for a more integrated railway system and better interstate rail connections was not great. But as the rapid settlement of the frontier continued and when, with the onset of the Civil War, the West began sending a veritable flood of food and animal products eastward and importing manufactured products in exchange, the demand for cheap and expeditious through shipment by rail over long distances became irresistible. Shippers of western products sought favorable rates without preference for particular cities or their captive railroads. Similarly, producers and distributers of manufactured products outgrew the nearby market and began to see the prospects of a national outlet for their products. Isolated railroads which had seemed earlier to offer the advantage of a protected market, now came to be regarded as barriers to profitable commercial relations with more distant areas.[6]

At the same time that the market was expanding so prodigiously, the attitude toward railroads as an investment underwent a substantial change. At least until some time in the fifties, funds for railroad development, as we have seen, had come chiefly from local sources, whether private or public. The incentive for investment was less the hope of direct returns from the railroads themselves than a belief that indirect benefits would inure to local producers, property owners, and merchants. During the fifties and increasingly thereafter, the motive for investment shifted more and more to a desire for direct returns: for profits derived from the issue or purchase of railroad securities and from railroad promotion, consolidation, and security manipulation. This development was accompanied by the rise of strong financial interests, especially in Boston and New

York, the growth of stock exchanges and specialized banking institutions, and the emergence of so-called "finance capitalism." Both investors and promoters, now looking far beyond the local market areas, sought the profits to be gained from the railroad lines which benefited any part of the continent.

There were indeed many facets to the evolution of an integrated system of railroad transportation in the United States and Canada. A full-length history of this development would cover at the very least: (1) the changes in the physical plant and equipment of the railroads, including both the adoption of uniform gauge and the improvement and standardization of techniques and equipment; (2) the evolution of institutional arrangements such as through bills of lading, agreements for the interline exchange of rolling stock, the adoption of standard time, consolidations, rate and traffic agreements, and the appearance of fast freight lines; and (3) the rapid growth of the whole economy, including the settlement of the West, the revolutionary changes in marketing, and the scale of industrial production.

Such a detailed study goes far beyond the scope of this volume. The intention here is a limited one. Only one aspect of the technological changes will be discussed: the adoption of a uniform gauge. The basic importance of this development can hardly be overemphasized, for the adoption of a uniform gauge hastened the closing of gaps between railroad lines at important junction cities, encouraged interline agreements on such matters as through bills of lading and passenger tickets, the division of through rates, and the exchange of rolling stock, and soon made necessary the adoption of standardized braking and coupling equipment. There is no attempt to examine in detail the history of the developments corollary to gauge standardization, but we have noted the pressures, chiefly the expansion of the market, which promoted this uniformity of gauge. In this connection, one particular institutional development, the growth of fast freight lines in response to market needs, is singled out for special attention.

7

II

THE RAILROAD MAP, 1861

CONSTRUCTION OF THE RAILROAD MAP

Maps which show the spread of the railroad net — often decade by decade — are used so commonly in the study of American railroad history that their presence in a book on the subject is taken for granted. The effectiveness of this type of visual aid, together with that of such other devices as charts, graphs, and pictographs also frequently used by social scientists, cannot be questioned. Yet, useful as these tools are, they can frequently confuse rather than clarify. Most students have become aware of the errors which may spring from an uncritical reading of charts and pictographs. Less well-recognized, however, are the similar dangers which may be encountered when using maps, for, wholly without intent, the manner in which a map is drawn may give the general reader, or even the historian, erroneous impressions and cause him to come to unwarranted conclusions.

A map is, of course, a much simplified picture which tells a story. This is never the whole story but merely a significant piece for the date indicated. For example, a good map showing the railroads of the United States for 1900 or 1950 may prove very useful for showing the extent and location of railroad lines in those years and for indicating the main routes of internal commerce. A similar map for 1860 may make possible an interesting comparison of the extent and location of the railroads that existed in the earlier and later periods. But if the reader assumes that the map dated 1860 shows the possible routes by rail for through movement of internal trade, as do the 1900 and 1950 maps, then his reading of the earlier map promotes error rather than understanding of the actual situation portrayed. When railroads are practically all of one gauge, physically united by interconnecting tracks, and so managed that the rolling stock of one road is permitted freely to pass over the tracks of another, the railroad map provides much useful information about possible traffic movement. But those conditions were not fulfilled until well after the Civil War, and for this reason railroad maps for the prewar period are often unsatisfactory and even misleading.

The three chapters immediately following this one emphasize the lack of physical integration of the railroads in the United States and Canada on the eve of the Civil War. Maps showing this condition and representing as accurately as possible the railroad net as it existed on April 1, 1861, appear at the end of this book. They indicate the extent and location, the position of the chief junction and terminal cities, and the rail gauge of each railroad.

If the maps are to be read profitably, brief attention must be given first to the condition of their preparation. The choice of the date, April 1, 1861, is somewhat arbitrary, but it has the advantage of presenting the picture of the American railroad network just before the actual outbreak of hostilities between the North and South.[1] The Civil War provides a convenient dividing point in American railway history, for during that conflict new construction was curtailed appreciably and thereafter a great new period of expansion and consolidation began.

The maps show railroads in operation. For the purposes of this study, a railroad considered to be in operation was one over which persons or commodities were transported for commercial purposes; that is, the railroad company received payment in return for its transportation services, or it carried commodities of its own production (for example, coal) not merely for its own use, but for sale. Thus, a newly built section of track which was used solely to transport materials needed for further construction, or upon which an excursion train was run to carry company officials and leading citizens to celebrate the "opening" of the road, was not, under the definition here adopted, regarded as actually in operation.

Furthermore, although the accompanying maps show in some detail the network of railroads in operation as of April 1, 1861, no serious attempt was made to include railroads of less than about ten miles in length. In the interest of simplicity two other omissions were made. Double-track lines were not indicated as such. These were located largely in New England and the Middle Atlantic States, where the maps already tended to be most congested. Secondly, although the maps indicate gauge differences and show breaks wherever major waterways remained unbridged, they do not show gaps in cities where lines remained unconnected. Nor, needless to say, do they give any indication of important institutional impediments to through traffic, which existed along with the physical discontinuities of the rail network.

SOURCES OF MAP INFORMATION

The chief obstacle to constructing an accurate railroad map for 1861 arose from the difficulty of securing reliable information. It was soon discovered that contemporary maps, though helpful, are never entirely trustworthy. Their inaccuracies arise, in part, from errors in execution and, in part, from the mapmakers' lack of data. But equally serious is their obscurity. It is not always clear whether the railroads shown on the maps are those that were actually in operation, or whether the maps also include roads that were in the course of construction, or merely projected. And, finally, the date of a given map is seldom definite; for it may mean merely that the map was printed in that year on the basis of data collected some time before, or it may indicate the situation at the beginning, the end, or on some intermediate day during the year.

The best of the contemporary railroad maps were published in the railway guides. These were printed and sold by a number of commercial publishers and issued annually, monthly, or even twice a month. They provided passenger timetables for most operating railroads. The most detailed and dependable information for constructing the maps in this volume came from the material contained in the railroad guides. They are remarkably complete, although information on newly opened or minor roads is sometimes missing. In some cases, the guides gave the date on which the train schedule was received from the individual railroad company. Unless clear evidence appeared to the contrary, this was accepted as proof that a railroad line was in actual operation on that date.

Of the general guides available those consulted chiefly were: *Dinsmore's Railroad and Steam Navigation Guide for the United States, Canada*, etc., and *Appleton's Railway and Steam Navigation Guide*. For New England, *The Pathfinder Railway Guide for the New England States* contains unusually reliable maps.[2] Of the other maps used for the period

10

under consideration the most useful were those published by J. H. Colton and Company of New York City.

Railroad journals and other commercial publications furnished information on the opening of new lines. But since the news items in these publications could be based on optimistic reports sent in by company officials, who were not unaware of the effect of such publicity on the reputation of the company, these media had to be used with caution. Annual reports of the railroad corporations, occasionally useful, were on the whole disappointing. The limitations of time and energy did not permit an extensive investigation and use of collections of correspondence, legislative records, personal memoirs, and newspapers, although such sources were consulted on disputed or obscure points whenever possible.

Finally, a word must be said concerning secondary sources. State and local histories, especially the latter, proved helpful in a few cases. Most valuable, of course, were the more scholarly regional and company railroad histories. Besides providing corroborative evidence on difficult points, they frequently directed the authors' attention to original materials which might otherwise have been overlooked. Almost without exception, the texts of these studies proved much more reliable than the maps which accompany them, for the maps are all too often poorly drafted, and are inaccurate and vague. Some of the very best railroad histories contain contemporary maps which are not even dated.[3]

REPRESENTATION OF GAUGES

One of the chief purposes of the maps appearing in this chapter is to show gauge differences as clearly as possible. By "gauge" is meant the distance between the rails measured from inside to inside. The major gauges are identifiable on the map by different colors or symbols. Very small variations in gauge, fairly common in 1861, are not indicated. Thus, while the standard gauge was normally 4 feet 8½ inches, individual roads regarded as standard-gauge roads at the time might vary from this width by at least ½ inch, and such a deviation was not considered a serious obstacle to through shipment.[4] The *Tenth Census of the United States*, 1880, stated that "the gauges from 4 feet 9⅜ inches to 4 feet 8 inches (both inclusive) may be considered standard, as rolling stock used upon either is interchanged without objection."[5]

Comprehensive and detailed information on railroad gauges has never been compiled and is extremely difficult to obtain.[6] Even when located such data are not always dependable and so far as possible must be checked against that in other sources. The gauges indicated on the maps here are believed to be correct, but in a few cases a decision about a gauge width had to be made on the basis of inadequate and sometimes conflicting records.[7] The chief sources for information on gauges are the contemporary railroad directories which were published annually and indicate the gauges for many of the railroads of the United States and Canada.[8] Although generally reliable, the directories contain occasional inaccuracies which can be discovered only by comparing them with each other and with other data available. Aside from what is contained in these publications, information is extremely scattered and must be sought in contemporary annual railroad reports and other railroad records, state reports, railroad and business periodicals, newspapers, and travel accounts.

GAUGE DIFFERENCES

When railroads were first constructed, their engineers experimented with different gauges. Each engineer tended to select the gauge which he thought best suited the needs of his particular road. Early British tramways had been built to varying gauges — as narrow as 3 feet 4 inches to as wide as 4 feet 6 inches.[9] Benjamin H. Latrobe, reporting to Albert Gallatin in 1808, suggested that railroads might be built with a distance of 3½ to 5 feet between the rails.[10] When George Stephenson built his successful steam railroad in England, he finally settled on a gauge of 4 feet 8½ inches. He was probably influenced in his choice by the English tramway and wagon gauges, but different writers present a number of explanations for his selection of exactly 4 feet 8½ inches.[11] Most of the early British railroads adopted this gauge, but some experimented with other widths, the most important deviations being those of 5 feet and 7 feet. The latter gauge was adopted by the Great Western on the advice of its engineer, Isambard Kingdom Brunel, a fanatical advocate of the broad gauge. The whole gauge controversy came to a head in Great Britain in 1845 when a Royal Commission was appointed to study the matter. The commission, reporting in 1846, recommended that in all future railroad construction a 4 foot 8½-inch gauge be used, and an Act of Parliament was passed to this effect.[12] Throughout Europe generally, the early railroads were built to this gauge. But there were exceptions.

In Ireland, 5 feet 3 inches was adopted after some experimentation. And on the continent examples of early deviant gauges are the Basle and Strassburg lines, with a width of 6 feet 3 inches, and the line from Ghent to Antwerp, which had a gauge of 3 feet 9 inches. By 1860 the prevailing gauge in Spain was 5 feet 6 inches and Russia's Moscow line was 6 feet.[13]

In the United States all the early railroads in New England as well as some of those in the Middle Atlantic States adopted the "Stephenson gauge" of 4 feet 8½ inches. They appear to have been following the British example, a course which may have been encouraged by the importation and use of Stephenson locomotives. But Stephenson engines were made to order to whatever gauge was specified, and many of the early locomotives used on American lines were manufactured in the United States. An unsigned article in *The American Railway Times*[14] offers another explanation for the adoption of the standard gauge in the United States. This article is worth quoting because it includes a plausible explanation for the adoption of another popular early American gauge, that of 4 feet 10 inches.

In the early history of railways in America they were laid with timbers running lengthwise with strips of iron, 3½ inches wide, nailed or spiked on the top for the wheels to run upon; they were of 5 feet guage, measuring from centre to centre of the iron or strap rail, as it was called; hence the origin of the 4 feet 8½ inch guage. At a later date, when the solid iron rail was introduced, it was with a two inch face also, the five foot guage measuring from centre to centre of rails; hence the origin of the 4 feet 10 inch guage; hence the conclusion, that if our system of measuring from inside to inside of the rails had been adopted at first, the uniform guage of this country would have been five feet, instead of being overrun with so many different guages, and such an enormous expense of reloading and changing cars, besides a great many other disadvantages attending the break of guages.

As has been shown, early American railroad promoters looked upon the railroad as primarily a means for short-haul transportation, and therefore saw little need for uniformity of railroad gauge. But there were those who from the first decade of the railroad-building era stressed the desirability of a national standard gauge not only from the standpoint of the cost and convenience of handling traffic but also for military reasons.[15] Engineers disagreed, however, about what was the most desirable gauge,[16] and mercantile interests stimulated the deliberate adoption of divergent gauges.

The general gauge situation as it existed on April 1, 1861, may be seen on the accompanying maps and will be commented upon for each section of the country in the chapters which follow. The statistics on gauges as they were reported on January 1, 1861, are shown in the following table.

RAILROAD MILEAGE BY GAUGES IN THE UNITED STATES AND CANADA, JANUARY 1, 1861 [a]

Number of railroad companies	Miles of road	Gauge	Percentage of total mileage
14	1,777	6′ 0″	5.3
21	2,896	5′ 6″	8.7
2	182	5′ 4″	.1 —
63	7,267	5′ 0″	21.8
39	3,294	4′ 10″	9.9
1	120	4′ 9¼″	.1 —
210	17,712	4′ 8½″	53.3

[a] *American Railway Times*, 13:186 (May 11, 1861). The same data appear in *The Merchant's Magazine*, 44:672 (May 1861), where it is also stated that most street railways had a gauge of 4 feet 8½ inches or 4 feet 10 inches, although those of Philadelphia were 5 feet 2½ inches.

III

NEW ENGLAND AND CANADA, 1861

SPOKES TO THE HUB

By 1861 no part of America was more adequately provided with railroads than southern New England. In northern New England also, in Vermont, New Hampshire, and Maine, substantial progress had been made in railway construction (see Map I at end). Early railroad maps give a more accurate picture of the railway network in this section of the country than in other areas, for here, with but one or two exceptions, the gauge of the roads was standard. Only the main line of the Grand Trunk, which angled from Portland across New Hampshire and Vermont, and some of the roads in the state of Maine, were of divergent gauges. Moreover, most of New England's rivers had been satisfactorily bridged and actual physical connections had been effected at appropriate junction points even between rival railroads.

A gauge of 4 feet 8½ inches was adopted by the first three railroads built in New England: the Boston and Lowell, the Boston and Worcester, and the Boston and Providence. Each of these roads imported Stephenson engines constructed for use on tracks of standard gauge. This set the pattern for southern New England, for with Boston capital playing a dominant role in most New England railroad construction, no serious consideration appears to have been given to the adoption of any other gauge. Moreover, as the railroads of eastern New York were of standard gauge, the New York City interests which had helped to supply capital for the railroads extending northward into western New England naturally favored that gauge.

Compared to the railroads in other sections of the country, those of New England were not only well unified internally, but were also relatively free from gaps or obstructions at points of intersectional connection. Traffic between New York City and Boston via New Haven, Hartford, and Springfield moved without physical obstacle over tracks owned by four different companies. By 1861 most of this route had been double tracked and though the usual disputes arose over the division of through rates and the need was recognized for systematizing the exchange of cars among the different companies, traffic moved without serious hindrance.[1] The shore line via New Haven and Providence provided an alternate route between New York and Boston. But it was inferior to the more inland one as bridges had not yet been erected at the mouths of either the Connecticut or Thames Rivers. When car ferries were finally installed at Lyme and New London late in 1859, through shipment was greatly facilitated.[2]

Boston's chief bid for intersectional commerce — the way by which it hoped to tap the rich trade of the West — was its direct line to the Hudson River via the Boston and Worcester and the Western Railroad. This route had a weak link at its western terminus, for there was no bridge across the river at Albany. A ferry helped to solve this problem during part of the year but even this substitute failed when winter ice closed the river. The failure to erect a bridge at Albany was caused by the efforts of the merchants of Troy to keep for their own city as much of the western trade as possible. First by successful pressure on the New York State legislature and then by obstructive court action, the Trojan business interests delayed the building of the Albany bridge until after the Civil War.[3]

Dissatisfied with their Albany connection and jealous of the traffic carried from the Lake region by the Erie Canal, the Hudson River, and the New York railroads, Boston interests sought a more independent link with the West. This they secured during the fifties by what came to be known as the Great Northern Route. Several railroads led northwestward from Boston toward White River Junction, Vermont, from whence, over three connecting lines, the route proceeded across the northern reaches of Lake Champlain and westward to Ogdensburg on the St. Lawrence, not far from the eastern end of Lake Ontario.

Though great things were expected of it, this route never proved a very strong competitor for the trade of the West. The individual companies quarreled over the division of the through rate, and the roadbed and equipment of the Vermont sector of the line were inadequate. Even though the Welland Canal, which permitted lake vessels to pass from Lake Erie to Lake Ontario, was enlarged, it still did not accommodate the largest lake vessels nor offer economies sufficient to divert much traffic from more southern outlets. Also, the traffic which did arrive on Lake Ontario might continue by river to Montreal.

The Northern Route, for a time, secured some of the traffic from the Upper Lakes via the Northern Railway of Canada. This line, completed in the middle fifties, permitted the movement of goods over the relatively short distance from Collingwood on Georgian Bay and across the Ontario Peninsula to Toronto and thence by Lake Ontario to Ogdensburg. This route carried considerable tonnage for a few years, but it was far from satisfactory.[4]

It should also be noted that the Great Northern Route made connection at Rouses Point with the Montreal and Champlain Railway, which led northward to Montreal, thus providing an uninterrupted rail line of standard gauge between the Atlantic and the St. Lawrence. But through movement beyond Montreal was impossible because the other roads leading from that city had a rail width of 5 feet 6 inches, a gauge for which the enterprising merchants of Portland, Maine, were largely responsible.

PORTLAND'S BID FOR RAILROAD EMPIRE

With its ice-free harbor, Portland, given the ocean transportation then available, was half a day closer to British ports than was Boston. Portland's merchants aspired to make their city a major exporting point for the produce of the Great Lakes region by achieving a direct connection with projected Canadian railroads. The business interests of Montreal, leading commercial city of Canada, preferred to trade directly with Europe via the St. Lawrence, but as this avenue was closed by ice during part of the year, they sought a satisfactory winter outlet. Boston merchants, of course, eagerly courted the Canadians and urged the Canadian railroads to adopt the standard gauge so that through shipment to the Massachusetts port would be possible by the Great Northern Route. But the greater distance to the more southerly port, the fear that Boston interests with their independent western connections on the Hudson and at Ogdensburg would prove less allies than rivals, and the importunities of persuasive spokesmen for the Maine city, led the merchants on the St. Lawrence to favor an alliance with Portland.[5]

Backed by municipal credit and prodded by that indefatigable railroad promoter, John Alfred Poor, Portland interests had succeeded in building the Atlantic and St. Lawrence Railroad westward from their city across New Hampshire and Vermont to the Canadian border. Here their line joined the St. Lawrence and Atlantic Railroad, a Montreal project built with substantial help from the Canadian government. Soon after construction was completed in 1853, both roads were taken over by the Grand Trunk Railway of Canada. When, in 1860, the Victoria Bridge spanning the St. Lawrence at Montreal was finished, Portland had not only a direct rail connection with Montreal but also with the Grand Trunk line which extended westward all the way to Sarnia on the St. Clair River opposite Port Huron, Michigan.

By 1861 Portland had achieved the best intersectional railroad connection of any American city. With no change of gauge or gaps in the line caused by waterways or city barriers, and under the auspices of only one railroad company, trains moved freely without breaking bulk over a route about 800 miles long. The city of Portland was at the eastern end of the longest railroad owned by a single company in the world, and for a time her trade benefited appreciably.[6]

Portland's venture in railroad building provides a typical example of the limited outlook of merchant capitalism. As early as 1843 Portland and Boston had been connected by a series of standard-gauge railroads financed largely by Boston promoters. Portland's commercial interests might well have regarded this as an advantageous development had they not, bemused by grandiose plans for the future of their own city as a leading ocean port, feared that Boston would capture their trade and make them merely a satellite city. Therefore, while providing themselves with an uninterrupted route to the west, the Portland merchants sought means to prevent Boston traders from sharing the expected benefits. If no preventive steps were taken, what was to keep the grasping Hub merchants from diverting the expected flow of western products from Portland's piers and bringing it to Boston wharves via their own railroads which extended southward from Portland? In order to forestall any such development, the charter secured by the Atlantic and St. Lawrence from the Maine legislature provided that the legislature could authorize rail-

18

road connections with this road "only on the easterly side." [7] The directors of the company took the further precaution of choosing a 5 foot 6-inch gauge for their road, thereby preventing through shipment from Canada to Boston without change of bulk. By agreement with the Canadian interests the gauge of the St. Lawrence and Atlantic, which extended from Montreal to the Vermont border, was also 5 feet 6 inches. This set the gauge pattern for the whole Grand Trunk system.

The promoters of the Portland–Montreal line attempted to justify to the public their selection of the broad gauge, a report by the chief engineer of The St. Lawrence and Atlantic Railroad making an elaborate effort to this end. Printed in Portland for distribution in pamphlet form, the statement stressed the technical advantages claimed for the broad gauge: improved performance by the locomotive; a lower center of gravity for rolling stock; the lessening of resistance on curves derived from the use of shorter trains; decreased danger of accident because of greater steadiness of the cars in motion; and the roominess of the passenger cars. Many of these technical points were still matters of serious dispute among the engineers of that time, but the pamphlet must have stretched the credulity of its readers even in that day when it stated that the transfer of passengers, which would be necessary at points where the gauge changed to another width, would be positively advantageous because it would add to the variety of the trip without adding to the passengers' inconvenience, and because it would permit a change from dusty cars to well-cleaned and ventilated ones. [8]

These claims were very largely window dressing. The main reason for adopting the wide gauge was clearly reflected at every stage. Poor, writing in 1848, declared: "The state of Maine, from its geographical position, has, naturally, less connection with the neighboring States than with the British Provinces. Her railway system, now partially developed, based upon the natural laws of trade, has but few relations to the other railways of New England, and has been projected upon a plan of complete independence to them all." [9] When rumors were afloat in 1860 that Boston interests might lay a third rail on their standard-gauge road leading southward from Portland so as to move broad-gauge cars directly to their wharves, the Maine legislature at the behest of Portland merchants promptly passed an act prohibiting these railroads from changing their gauge or adding a third rail without the express permission of the legislature, but this restriction did not apply to railroads east of Portland. The law was entitled "An act to promote safety of travel on railroads," but no one was deceived as to its real purpose.[10]

The adoption of the wide gauge by the Atlantic and St. Lawrence brought to the state of Maine a legacy of mixed gauges. (See Map I at end.) The same interests that backed the Atlantic and St. Lawrence were also behind the building of two other Maine roads of similar gauge, the Androscoggin and Kennebec and the Penobscot and Kennebec. The first was built eastward from Danville, which was on the Atlantic and St. Lawrence Railroad, to Waterville, and the second on beyond Waterville to Bangor. At Bangor a "connection" was made with the standard-gauge Bangor, Old Town and Milford, which had been built largely by Boston capital and was one of the oldest railroads in the state.

Important Maine cities which were not on the broad-gauge line, such as the capital city, Augusta, had their own hopes of becoming railroad centers and resented the activities of the Portland broad-gauge enthusiasts led by Poor. With the aid of Boston capital, they constructed a standard-gauge railroad. This followed the coast eastward from Portland to the Kennebec River, and there turning northward, passed through Augusta, crossed the broad-gauge line at Waterville, and went on to Skowhegan. The standard-gauge line had the great advantage of being able to exchange rolling stock at Portland with the Portland, Saco and Portsmouth, which ran to the southwest along the coast and connected with lines leading to Boston. The struggle between the backers of the broad-gauge roads and the standard-gauge ones was continuous. At Portland and Waterville, the two roads refused to facilitate the transfer of passengers and freight between their lines until forced to do so by legislative action. Maine, then, was the one New England state which, until some years after the Civil War, suffered from an uncoördinated railroad system.[11]

MONTREAL AND THE CANADIAN SYSTEM

In Canada, the business leaders of Montreal were even more dominant in their area than were the Boston merchants in New England. The result was that Canada had by 1861 a remarkably well-integrated railroad system. Backed by British capital, and with influence sufficient to secure favorable charters as well as substantial financial aid from the Canadian government, the Montreal interests were able to prevent the creation of serious artificial obstacles to railroad traffic within the province. The earliest Canadian railroads, which used Stephenson engines, were built to standard gauge, as were those of New England. But the decision, influenced by Portland, to construct the St. Lawrence and Atlantic to a 5 foot 6-inch gauge committed the Montreal promoters to building their railroads to that width. Not only did they construct the Grank Trunk to the wide gauge, but they made sure also that other important Canadian roads were so built, including the Great Western of Canada which stretched from the Suspension Bridge at Niagara to Windsor opposite Detroit.

The American lines which later combined to form the New York Central invested about $500,000 in the stock of the Great Western. The New York Central group, which was interested in this direct route to Detroit and Chicago, and whose railroads were built to the width of 4 feet 8½ inches, insisted that that gauge be adopted for the Great Western. But the powerful Montreal–Grand Trunk interests brought sufficient pressure, through their connections with the Canadian government, to force the Great Western to lay its rails to the 5 foot 6-inch gauge.[12]

The suggestion has sometimes been made that the Canadian government adopted the broad gauge as a defense measure, believing it would make invasion from the United States more difficult. No documentary confirmation of this theory has come to the attention of the authors, but this argument was used at times as a justification for the adoption of the variant gauge. A leading Canadian railroad authority, writing in 1862, urged that the building of a railroad westward from Montreal to Lake Huron was desirable on military grounds and regarded the broad gauge as a protective device against possible American depradations.[13]

The gauge differences which did appear in Canada were not seriously disruptive of internal trade. The two standard-gauge roads north of the St. Lawrence, the Ottawa and Prescott and the St. Lawrence and Industry, were primarily engaged in moving lumber from the interior down to the river for loading onto barges, and they operated only in the summertime. The two standard-gauge roads leading southward from Montreal were merely extensions of roads of similar gauge from below the border. By 1861 Canada had 1881 miles of railroad in operation. Only

147 miles were standard gauge. The remainder had the so-called "Canadian gauge" of 5 feet 6 inches.[14]

As the reader may see from Map I, a beginning had been made by 1861 on railroad building in the Maritime Provinces, with the standard gauge established in Nova Scotia and the 5 foot 6-inch width in New Brunswick. Although the Grand Trunk had reached Rivière du Loup on the St. Lawrence, it was not until well after the American Civil War that either this line or extensions of the Maine railroads made contact with those of the Maritime Provinces.[15]

Except for the road to Portland, Maine, the uniformly wide gauge within Canada formed an artificial hindrance to trade across the border. Montreal was connected by rail with both New York and Boston, but by standard-gauge roads, which made interchange of rolling stock at the Canadian city impossible. At the Niagara gateway the Suspension Bridge brought standard-gauge cars onto Canadian soil, but there all freight had to be transferred to rolling stock built to a 5 foot 6-inch gauge. At Fort Erie, Ontario, the cars of the Buffalo and Lake Huron Railway crossed the Niagara River on "the Company's Floating Steam Bridge"[16] but could proceed no further because of the gauge difference. Similar obstacles hindered through movement of traffic to the westward. The Great Western operated a steam car ferry between Windsor and Detroit, but as Michigan railroads were of standard width, no exchange of rolling stock was possible. At Sarnia the Grand Trunk made use of a ferry to Port Huron, Michigan, and leased the American line running from Port Huron to Detroit, but the difference in gauge required a change of bulk at Port Huron.[17]

IV

THE MIDDLE ATLANTIC STATES, 1861

NEW YORK'S THREE SYSTEMS

If both New England and Canada had internal railroad networks which were at least fairly well integrated, the same cannot be said for the Middle Atlantic States. There, merchants in the chief competing centers, New York, Philadelphia, and Baltimore, fought to establish autonomous railroad empires. They opposed connections between their own roads and those which led to rival ports, and introduced gauge differences to secure transportation monopolies in their expanding hinterlands. The result was a very different railroad pattern from that of southern New England.

Benefiting from the completion of the Erie Canal in 1825, and enjoying the most rapidly growing foreign trade in the country, the merchants of New York City were slow at first to recognize the vital role which the railroads might play. But once convinced of the feasibility of the new method of transportation, and alarmed at the successful pioneering with steam railroads by Boston and Baltimore, New Yorkers began in the 1840's to create their own railroad empire. By 1861 they had surpassed all their rivals in the extent to which they had bound to themselves by iron rails not only the nearby countryside but especially the rich back country toward the west. They accomplished this by establishing three great rail systems which were largely shut off from through connections with lines terminating in rival cities. The roads which converged on New York were "systems" in the sense that they had for the most part a uniform

23

gauge, thus permitting interchange of rolling stock where advantageous, but not in the sense that there was common ownership or operation. The period when many small railroad lines were consolidated into larger companies had only just begun, although it may be noted that it had already gone farther in central New York than in any other part of the country.

Each of the three systems was of a different gauge. The most extensive, of standard gauge, consisted of two lines east of and paralleling the Hudson River from New York City to Albany; a line (the New York Central) which extended across the state from Albany to Buffalo; and the lines connecting with this railroad to the northward of its main stem.[1] This network was made up for the most part of relatively short roads which had been constructed under the sponsorship of local commercial and agricultural interests. With the exception of the Mohawk and Hudson, which was largely a New York City project, the ten short lines which had been consolidated in 1853 to form the New York Central Railroad had been promoted and financed chiefly by merchants in the growing commercial centers — on or not far from the Erie Canal. For example, the Auburn and Syracuse Railroad was originally financed by the business interests of its two terminal cities, even though much of its stock soon came to rest in the strong boxes of New York City investors. The Schenectady and Troy Railroad was a full-fledged municipal enterprise, constructed to promote the commercial interests of Troy and financed by that city's government.[2]

In the 1850's, these railroads became feeders for the port of New York, for the produce they carried to Troy and Albany proceeded in large part down the Hudson, or via one of the two railroads east of the river to New York City. The two lines east of the Hudson River, the Hudson River Railroad and the Harlem Railroad, had been built by New York promoters and, despite the lack of a bridge at Albany, formed an important link in New York's chain of control over the inland trade.

Even though the standard-gauge[3] railroad system of New York was for the most part originally built by local interests, it was presently captured by and made tributary to New York City merchants and their allies. The New York and Erie Railroad, on the other hand, was from the beginning a New York project. It was built from Piermont on the Hudson to Dunkirk on Lake Erie and was the longest railroad under single ownership when completed across the state in 1851. This line was promoted by New York interests in order to secure the trade of the southern tier of counties and also to acquire for the metropolis a second through route to the Great Lakes. The merchants and farmers of the southern counties were eager to have a railroad and assisted with their capital and with their influence in the legislature, thereby helping to obtain substantial financial aid from the state.

So concerned were the promoters of the New York and Erie road that their city should monopolize the resultant trade, that they not only had the line built to the unusual gauge of six feet, but they also accepted a provision in the charter to the effect that the charter itself should be forfeited if the Erie made connection with any railroad leading into Ohio, Pennsylvania, or New Jersey.[4] The unusually wide gauge, it is true, was decided upon in the 1830's when engineers in both England and the United States were still debating the relative advantages of different gauges, and the chief engineer of the Erie believed sincerely in the desirability of the broad gauge. Nevertheless, the president of the Erie, Eleazar Lord, along with his mercantile associates in New York City, was undoubtedly interested in building a road which could not aid the commercial ambitions of any rival port.[5] The original terminals of the Erie were not well chosen, but by 1861 an outlet had been secured at Buffalo in the west and at Jersey City in the east. In addition to its main line, the Erie's broad gauge reached northward to make contact at strategic points with the New York Central system.

To the south other broad-gauge railroads extended into Pennsylvania and New Jersey. The chief one of these was the Delaware, Lackawanna and Western Railroad. Starting from Great Bend it angled through the coal country of northeast Pennsylvania and on into New Jersey where it joined the Jersey Central at New Hampton. From there, first on the Jersey Central and then on the New Jersey Railroad, the broad-gauge cars of the Lackawanna were carried by means of a third rail all the way through to Jersey City.[6]

The third system which fed traffic into the port of New York was made up of the railroads of northern New Jersey. This network was not as completely under New York control as were the Erie and New York Central systems and it suffered from some confusion of gauges, but one important line in the northern part of the state, the New Jersey Central, was standard gauge. Through its connection with the Lehigh Valley Railroad, it permitted exchange of rolling stock with the Pennsylvania railroads and, via Harrisburg and Pittsburgh, gave New York what amounted to a third rail route to the West.[7]

Except for the New Jersey Central and the broad-gauge roads reaching southward from the Erie, most of the Jersey railroads had a rail width of 4 feet 10 inches, known as the "New Jersey gauge." This gauge had been originally adopted by the earliest major railroad in the state, the Camden and Amboy. The reasons for the selection of the slightly divergent width of track are not entirely clear, but once having been adopted, it was accepted for most of the railroads in the state.

Built largely by business interests in the cities on the lines, the railroads of northern New Jersey furnished an important tidewater outlet for Pennsylvania coal and New Jersey farm produce.

PHILADELPHIA'S RAILROAD DOMAIN

The Pennsylvania railroads of 1861 may be separated into two divisions: (1) those in the eastern part of the state, north and northwest of Philadelphia, which were for the most part anthracite roads; and (2) those which led westward and were designed to give Philadelphia control of the trade of the Susquehanna Valley and western Pennsylvania, as well as to provide, via Pittsburgh, an avenue of commerce with the Ohio Valley.

Although mercantile influence was present, it was often subordinated to investor interests in the building of the anthracite railroads. The owners of the coal lands, who were Philadelphia and New York merchants in considerable part, promoted the building of the coal roads in the hope of raising the sale value of their property and in order to market their product as cheaply and efficiently as possible. Hence, the railroads which they financed led from the anthracite beds to Philadelphia and also northward to New York and eastward across New Jersey to New York harbor. Although most of these anthracite roads (including all of those leading into Philadelphia), were standard gauge, one important coal road, the Lackawanna, belonged to the broad-gauge system dominated by the Erie.

Philadelphia mercantile interests had not originally raised serious impediments to the two slight dips which the main Erie line made into Pennsylvania nor to the construction of the broad-gauge roads across

26

the northeast corner of their state which were to become the Lackawanna. But when they later awakened to the competition from this
direction, they induced their state legislature in 1852 henceforth to require all roads constructed in the state (except in a designated area along
the border of Ohio) to have a gauge of 4 feet 8½ inches.[8]

No attempt has been made to indicate on the map the intricate maze
of short coal lines in Pennsylvania. Many were solely or in part gravity
roads, designed merely to carry coal from the mine to the nearest water
transportation. They were occasionally of unusual gauge. Thus, the tracks
of both the Delaware and Hudson and the Pennsylvania Coal Company
were built to a 4 foot 3-inch gauge.[9]

The standard-gauge system, which led from Philadelphia into the
Susquehanna Valley by a number of routes and then by a single stem
to the western gateway at Pittsburgh, constituted Philadelphia's bid for
commercial preëminence. No gauge difference separated this railroad
system from that of Baltimore to the south, and Philadelphia merchants
repeatedly brought pressure to bear on their state legislature to prevent
connections with the Maryland railroads. They succeeded in delaying, but
ultimately failed to prevent, the building of the Baltimore-controlled
Northern Central Railroad from Baltimore up into the Susquehanna
Valley.[10] This strategic line gave Baltimore a share of the trade of central
Pennsylvania, effected a connection at Harrisburg with the Pennsylvania
Railroad's line to Pittsburgh, and through its extension to Sunbury in 1861
tapped the coal trade. The Northern Central, an unwelcome interloper
into Philadelphia territory, was finally tamed when it fell into financial
difficulties late in 1860 and came under the control of the Pennsylvania
Railroad.[11]

Philadelphia commercial interests were surprisingly slow to appreciate
the threat of the Baltimore and Ohio Railroad until in 1842 that line
reached Cumberland, Maryland, and sought a charter which would
permit it to build across southwestern Pennsylvania to Pittsburgh. Phila-
delphians now declared the Baltimore and Ohio Railroad a Baltimore
project, "designed for their aggrandizement by our impoverishment, and
enabling them to reap private advantages whilst they bear no portion of
the public burden." [12] To ward off this threat the Quaker City merchants
helped raise the money and secured a charter for the Pennsylvania Railroad, which was to extend from Harrisburg to Pittsburgh.[13] They lobbied

so successfully against the Baltimore and Ohio that it was prevented from securing a satisfactory charter from the state legislature. As a result, Baltimore's road had to be satisfied with an Ohio River terminus at Wheeling, Virginia. The influence of local merchants had again thwarted the pre-Civil War development of a coördinated railroad network.[14]

Pennsylvania's railway system was isolated to a considerable extent from the railroad lines of adjoining states; moreover, the city of Philadelphia, which appears from the railroad map to be a connecting point for intersystem lines, proved on the contrary to be a major obstacle to the through movement of passengers and freight. The Camden and Amboy Railroad terminated in Camden across the Delaware from Philadelphia. The tracks of the Philadelphia and Trenton, the other railroad which led to New York, extended no farther than Kensington, just north of Philadelphia. And, although the tracks of both the Pennsylvania and the Philadelphia, Wilmington and Baltimore railroads entered the city, they did not connect with each other or with the Philadelphia and Trenton line to the north. The only means of moving goods from any one of these three roads to another was by drays or horse cars drawn through congested city streets on poorly maintained rail lines owned by the street railway company.[15]

Only when under pressure from unusual demands for expeditious service during the Civil War, and when there was a threat in 1863 of a line to be federally subsidized and built from Washington, D. C. through to New York City, were arrangements finally made for connecting the railroads which terminated in Philadelphia. Various factors had contributed to the continuation of this anomalous situation; unquestionably, commercial cupidity played an important part. Thus a pamphleteer of Philadelphia wrote in 1862:

A strange misapprehension pervades the community, to the effect that a continuous line of railway between the North and Washington would detrimentally affect the interests of this city and make Philadelphia a mere wayside station.[16]

At the same time that Philadelphia merchants feared the outside competition which would result from through rail connections, New York merchants sought persistently to obtain a through rail route to Washington. The New York Chamber of Commerce stated in a communication to the United States Congress on December 5, 1861:

We believe they [those who shipped goods or travelled between New York and Philadelphia] are deprived, in an unjust and illiberal manner, of one of the most sacred rights of a free people — the right of a free and unrestricted highway for the transaction of every description of communication and public traffic. There can be, in the opinion of your memorialists, but one reason advanced for the principal broken links in this line of conveyance, that reason being unquestionably the local profit derived by the large towns on the route from the delay forced upon travellers by a compulsory stoppage in those places.[17]

Southward from Philadelphia, the Philadelphia, Wilmington and Baltimore extended to the city of Baltimore. But there was one break at the Susquehanna River. The road on both sides of the river was owned by a single company which by 1861 had instituted a car ferry for the transfer of both passenger and freight cars. The construction of a bridge there was delayed not so much by commercial jealousy as by expense and technical difficulties.[18]

BALTIMORE'S B AND O

Baltimore merchants were among the earliest in the United States to appreciate the commercial potentialities of the railroad. The first tracks of the Baltimore and Ohio were laid in 1829, although more than two decades passed before construction to the Ohio River was completed. By 1861 the city of Baltimore had become an important railroad center. The main line of the Baltimore and Ohio led to the Ohio River with terminals at Wheeling and Parkersburg; an extension of the same railroad ran from Baltimore to Washington; the Northern Central, as previously noted, reached up into the Susquehanna Valley of Pennsylvania, and, finally, the Philadelphia, Wilmington and Baltimore led directly to Philadelphia. Promoted and financed by business interests in Baltimore and helped repeatedly by both the city and the state, the Baltimore and Ohio and the Northern Central were the fighting weapons of Baltimore commerce and were generally recognized as such. A speaker before the Committee on Railroads of the Senate and Assembly of the State of New York in 1869 summed up the situation:

Both the Pennsylvania Central and Baltimore and Ohio Railroads, were built from motives of state and city policy. A profitable investment for capital was not the moving cause for the construction of either: they were constructed for the promotion of the interests of their respective States and cities where they terminate. Their destiny cannot be fulfilled, excepting by taking to their cities a large share of the trade of the West.[19]

The railroad situation at Baltimore offered the same kind of obstacles to through shipment as those described for Philadelphia. The two railroads which entered the city from the north, the Northern Central and the Philadelphia, Wilmington and Baltimore, made no direct connection with each other or with the Baltimore and Ohio. Exchange of rolling stock among these railroads was possible only by using horses or mules to haul cars through the city streets on the tracks of the street railway system.[20] The Baltimore and Ohio had excellent terminal facilities which made possible the direct transfer of goods from vessel to freight car, for rails had been laid to the end of the pier in Baltimore harbor. The Baltimore terminal of the Northern Central Railroad, on the other hand, was still located over a mile from the harbor in 1861. There were obvious advantages to Baltimore and Ohio interests in keeping the Northern Central Railroad from a waterfront terminal, for by means of its connection with the Pennsylvania Railroad, the Northern Central competed for the western trade. Baltimore merchants sought to enlarge their western trade but they preferred that it move over a route which they owned and controlled themselves.[21]

BARRIERS AT WESTERN GATEWAYS: BUFFALO AND ERIE

The foregoing survey of the railroads of the Middle Atlantic States indicates the extent to which the systems dominated by the various ports were isolated from each other. Serious as were these hindrances to intrasectional trade, they were equaled or exceeded by the difficulties of through trade between the Middle Atlantic States and adjoining regions. This was least true of intercourse between New York and New England, for, even though the lack of a bridge over the Hudson at Albany was a real inconvenience, the railroads of New York east of the Hudson made direct connection with those of New England and no change of gauge was involved. Elsewhere, however, through rail movement between sections without change of bulk was impossible.

The need for a railroad from Buffalo, New York, to Cleveland, Ohio, which would connect the New York Central and the Erie Railroads with the railroads in the Lake States, was met early in the 1850's by the construction of four short connecting lines. These were: The Buffalo and

State Line whose location is indicated by its name; The Erie and North-East, which ran from the New York border to Erie; the line of the Franklin Canal Company which led from Erie to the Ohio border; and the Cleveland, Painesville and Ashtabula which completed the line to Cleveland. The second link in this line, the Erie and North-East Railroad, was the first to be completed. It was built with a 6-foot gauge in the expectation of connecting with an extension of the Erie and with the hope of later adding a third rail to provide a standard-gauge connection with the New York Central.

But the Erie was unable to extend its tracks to the state line because of financial difficulties, and presently Ohio and New York railroad interests combined to complete the other three links in the route between Buffalo and New York. These links were all of the Ohio gauge, 4 feet 10 inches, and made Buffalo the transfer point while giving no advantage to either the 6-foot Erie or the standard-gauge New York Central. In order to secure a through route of uniform 4 foot 10-inch gauge from Buffalo to Erie, the control of the Erie and North-East Railroad was secured by the management of the three other lines and plans were laid to convert it to the 4 foot 10-inch gauge.

This development alarmed the people of Erie and Harbor Creek, the two terminals of the broad-gauge Erie and North-East Railroad. The break in gauge had become a vested interest giving employment to labor and profit to food sellers and porters. Determined not to lose their advantage, the citizens of the area appealed to the Pennsylvania legislature to prevent the gauge change. That body, ever anxious to protect the commerce of Philadelphia and the interests of the Pennsylvania Railroad against New York competition, gave prompt assistance by passing a law (March 1851), which provided that railroads west of Erie should use the 4 foot 10-inch gauge and those east, 6 feet or 4 feet 8 ½ inches.[22]

This legislation was repealed the following year, possibly, as was charged, as the result of unusual activity by out-of-state pressure groups.[23] At any rate, disappointed but quite unwilling to admit defeat, the citizens of Erie and Harbor Creek then took matters into their own hands. Whenever work was begun on changing the gauge of the Erie and North-East, they tore up the tracks and destroyed bridges. The city council of Erie adopted an ordinance forbidding any change of gauge. Legal battles ensued and local officers of the law aided and abetted the mobs in destroying railroad property. Leading citizens joined in defying the United States Marshal who, on one occasion, was locked in the city jail. Public sentiment in Philadelphia appears to have supported Erie's defiance of the out-of-state railroad interests and the governor of Pennsylvania expressed his sympathy with the citizens of Erie.

The contest continued into 1856, the chief action taking place in the courts and the state legislature but with sporadic acts of violence whenever any attempt was made to change the six-foot gauge. Finally, the state took over control of the broad-gauge line. After prolonged bargaining, as a result of which the city of Erie and the state of Pennsylvania wrung costly concessions from the out-of-state railroad interests, the Erie and North-East Railroad was permitted to change the gauge of its rails to conform to the 4 foot 10-inch gauge of the rest of the route.[24]

The "War of the Gauges," was much more than a local Erie affair. In its larger aspects, it was a struggle between New York merchants, who sought improved connections with the Middle West, and Philadelphia businessmen, who were determined to discourage rivals of their own Pennsylvania Railroad. Spokesmen for New York attacked the dog-in-the-manger policy of the Philadelphia merchants and threatened to support federal measures that would overcome what they regarded as an illegal interference with interstate trade. They even let it be known that they might support national legislation designed to remove the federal mint from Philadelphia. The Philadelphia Board of Trade by unanimous vote denied any wish to interfere with legitimate commerce. But they roundly condemned "foreign [that is, New York] speculators" and expressed the hope that "the just rights of Erie may be fully maintained and completely protected against the grasping policy of certain railroad corporations who are unjustly interfering with their interests, and who will stop at no means to accomplish their ends." [25]

BARRIERS AT WESTERN GATEWAYS:
PITTSBURGH, WHEELING, AND PARKERSBURG

The Pennsylvania Railroad at Pittsburgh and the Baltimore and Ohio at Wheeling encountered the same gauge barrier as did their New York rivals at Buffalo. The Allegheny River had been bridged at Pittsburgh by the Pittsburgh, Fort Wayne and Chicago Railroad in 1857,[26] and by 1858 a connection had been made with the Pennsylvania Railroad at that city. The Fort Wayne line provided a 4 foot 10-inch route all the way to Chicago but a break of bulk was usually necessary at Pittsburgh because of gauge differences. In time a way was found to interchange rolling stock between railroads having a standard gauge and those built with the 4 foot 10-inch gauge.[27] In some cases, cars constructed to the 4 foot 8½-inch gauge were moved all the way from St. Louis to Philadelphia, despite the fact that from Indianapolis to Pittsburgh they traveled over rails built for rolling stock having a wheel spread of 4 feet 10 inches, but this practice never proved completely satisfactory.

For a short time after the Fort Wayne line had completed its bridge over the Allegheny and entered the city of Pittsburgh, its tracks stopped 200 feet short of those of the Pennsylvania. Local interests believed it to their advantage to do everything in their power to oppose the through movement of freight, and the merchants were supported by the mayor and the city council. But despite court orders and even with recourse to violence, Pittsburgh merchants were able to delay the closing of this gap for only a few months. They were not strong enough to defeat the demands of Philadelphia merchants and of the Pennsylvania Railroad Company for a through route to the West.[28]

At Wheeling, the Baltimore and Ohio faced the same gauge difficulty as the Pennsylvania Railroad at Pittsburgh, for the tracks of the Ohio Central, which terminated at Bellaire on the Ohio River opposite Wheeling, were built to a 4 foot 10-inch gauge. The transfer problem was even more serious here, however, than at Pittsburgh, for there was no railroad bridge across the Ohio, and passengers and freight alike had to be shuttled across the river.[29]

The Baltimore and Ohio, via the Northern Virginia Railroad, had a second connection with the West at Parkersburg, Virginia. From Belpre opposite Parkersburg, the Marietta and Cincinnati Railroad led to Cincinnati. But here again there was no through movement of trains before the Civil War, for, although the Marietta and Cincinnati like the Baltimore and Ohio was a standard-gauge road, there was no bridge across the Ohio until 1870 and car ferries were not used before 1867.[30]

Thus, on every rail route between the Middle Atlantic States and Ohio, gauge differences or unbridged rivers presented serious obstacles to the efficient transportation of passengers and freight. No wonder that the Erie Canal continued to offer effective competition until well after the

Civil War, and that the development of through railroad traffic was a disappointment to the hopes of railroad promoters in eastern cities. For the five years ending September 30, 1860, the percentage of total tonnage which represented through freight carried by each of three of the main routes was reported as follows: the Pennsylvania carried east 14 per cent, west 10½ per cent; the Baltimore and Ohio carried east 16⅝ per cent, west 7¼ per cent; and the New York Central carried east 25¼ per cent, west 5¾ per cent.[31]

V

THE MIDWEST AND SOUTH, 1861

Railroad construction in the Middle West had made hardly more than a beginning in the decade of the 1840's, and by 1850 total construction in this area equaled only about 1200 miles. But during the following decade more track was laid in this than in any other section of the country, with the result that by the outbreak of the Civil War the states north of the Ohio River were crisscrossed with many railroads, aggregating more than 10,000 miles of track. The Ohio and Mississippi Rivers were connected with the Great Lakes, and the larger cities on the two rivers were also joined by rail. Beyond the Mississippi, in Missouri and Iowa, the great building era was just getting under way; many lines were beginning to stretch out toward the West. One road, the Hannibal and St. Joseph, had reached the Missouri River. The era of actual construction in Minnesota had not yet begun.

The unity of the midwestern railroad net was marred by differences in gauge. The first Ohio railroad, the Mad River and Lake Erie, had a width of 4 feet 10 inches, because, it was said, its first locomotive, *The Sandusky*, which was acquired in New Jersey, was designed to operate on a track of that gauge.[1] Other early Ohio railroads copied this gauge, and the Ohio legislature passed a law on February 11, 1848, providing that all roads built within the state should have a 4 foot 10-inch gauge.[2] This law was modified appreciably in 1852 when the legislature, without prescribing a particular width, merely required that any railroad in Ohio should have "one uniform gauge or width of track from end to end."[3] Yet even before the passage of this act other gauges had been author-

35

ized; of two railroad charters granted in 1851, one permitted the Franklin and Warren Railroad to be constructed to a gauge necessary to conform to any railroad with which it might connect; and the other provided that the Ohio and Mississippi Railroad might lay its tracks to a 6-foot gauge.[4]

By 1861 the gauge pattern of Ohio had become more confused than that of any other state. Lines south of Lake Erie, leading from Cleveland to Toledo and westward, were built to the 4 foot 8½-inch width, as was the Marietta and Cincinnati in southern Ohio. The Fremont and Indiana in northern Ohio connected a standard-gauge road with a 4 foot 10-inch one but was itself constructed to the so-called "compromise gauge" of 4 feet 9¼ inches. Two lines, one southward from Sandusky and the other northward from Portsmouth on the Ohio, were constructed to the unusual width of 5 feet 4 inches. Finally, the broad-gauge Ohio and Mississippi led all the way from the Mississippi opposite St. Louis across southern Illinois and Indiana and terminated at Cincinnati, Ohio. This road, influenced by the Erie, was built to a 6-foot gauge throughout; a third rail was added from Cincinnati to Lawrenceburg in order to permit interchange of traffic with the standard-gauge Indianapolis and Cincinnati, which had its southern terminal at Lawrenceburg.

As may be seen from Map II, the pattern of railroad gauges in the Middle West was simplest in Michigan, Wisconsin, and Iowa, where all lines were standard gauge. Most of the Indiana railroads were also of standard gauge, but the Ohio influence is reflected in the 4 foot 10-inch lines which appear in the east and north. Moreover, the 6-foot Ohio and Mississippi Railroad crossed the southern part of the Hoosier State. In 1861 the Illinois section of the latter railroad was the only line in that state not of standard gauge. It is true that one other Illinois railroad, the Chicago and Elgin (later a part of the Northwestern system), originally had been built to the Erie width, but it had been changed to standard in June 1855.[5] The two gauges in Missouri indicate the border position of that state; in northern Missouri the railroads were standard gauge, like those of Iowa; in the southern part the 5 foot 6-inch gauge followed the Arkansas pattern.[6]

There is no indication that the confusion of railroad gauges in Indiana and Ohio was planned deliberately. It appears to have been merely carried over from the confused situation in the East. Engineers had reached no agreement on the most satisfactory gauge, and the first short lines constructed in the forties and early fifties were designed primarily to serve local needs. As the tempo of railroad construction increased during the middle fifties the unplanned confusion of gauges continued, although by the end of the decade the disadvantages were becoming manifest.

CITY RIVALRIES IN THE MIDWEST

City rivalries did not tend in Indiana and Ohio, as they often did in the East and South, to promote gauge differences or other impediments to through traffic. Rivalries were just as common in this region,[7] but only in one instance, the opposition to the bridging of the Ohio, do they appear to have resulted in any appreciable effort to restrain through movement of freight and passengers.

Before the Civil War the Ohio River presented a serious obstacle to east-west as well as to north-south trade, for no railroad crossed the river until a bridge was completed at Steubenville in 1862-63. Engineering difficulties and the large capital investment that was required help to account for this delay, especially on the lower reaches of the river. However, on the upper river commercial rivalries played a part. Pittsburgh shipping and steamboat interests strongly opposed any bridging of the Ohio. When a highway bridge was erected to Wheeling in 1849, they declared it a menace to navigation and conducted a prolonged court and legislative fight against it; a proposal for a railroad bridge across the Ohio at Steubenville was strongly opposed in Wheeling.[8]

With the foregoing exception, both local and outside pressures in Ohio and Indiana discouraged the development of restrictive policies against railroad development. It must be remembered that this was an area dominated by agriculture, and its prosperity depended in no small part on the cheapness and efficiency with which merchants were able to send raw materials to eastern markets and bring back processed goods. Even if the traders of a particular city had sought to capture this traffic by erecting barriers to through rail movement, they could not have done so effectively. The trade of no very appreciable area could be monopolized, for the rush of railroad building in the fifties had created alternate routes to the East, and additional lines could easily have been built through terrain which was relatively favorable to railroad construction.

In neither Ohio nor Indiana, nor for that matter elsewhere in the Midwest, were gaps in railroad lines deliberately created or maintained within city limits. In fact, through railroad connections in midwest cities were effected at a very early date in railroad development. In 1850 railroads entering Indianapolis completed the construction of the Union Track Railway; three years later these same companies had built the first union passenger station in the United States.[9]

A gap in rail transportation did exist, however, at Cincinnati. There the Little Miami Railroad, terminating in the eastern part of the city, made no connection with either the Indianapolis and Cincinnati or the Ohio and Mississippi, both of which entered from the west. Through East-West rail shipments had to be carted through the city streets from one terminal to the other until connecting tracks were finally laid down shortly before the end of the Civil War. Some local interests may have gained from the break in the line and this might have been a factor in its retention; but the persistence of this city gap appears to have been caused more by reluctance to make the necessary investment in a connection before a time when strong demand for through shipment arose.[10]

No less convinced than the people of Ohio and Indiana of the desirability of through railroad movement were the eastern interests which played an increasingly important role in western railroad development. The building of the early railroads in Ohio and Indiana had been largely a local venture and, for the most part, not a very profitable one. Therefore, when the eastern railroads reached Lake Erie and the Ohio River in the early fifties, and their promoters began looking for western connections, they found the roads in these states typically capital starved, poorly equipped, and often uncompleted over projected routes. By 1861 the New York Central, the Pennsylvania, and the Baltimore and Ohio, by furnishing capital and expert management, had greatly extended their influence over the Ohio and Indiana railroads and had developed traffic lines across the two states to the commercial centers farther west.

The New York Central group, as has already been shown, was active in promoting the construction of the lines both north and south of Lake Erie which connected with roads leading to Chicago. The Pennsylvania Railroad gave assistance to and gradually came to control the Pittsburgh, Fort Wayne and Chicago. Made up of a combination of short lines this 4 foot 10-inch road finally reached Chicago in 1858 and thereby provided a route of uniform gauge from Pittsburgh to Chicago.[11]

From the Ohio River opposite Wheeling the 4 foot 10-inch Central Ohio led westward and northwestward, and by connecting with roads of similar gauge reached Chicago, Indianapolis, and Cleveland. Both the Pennsylvania and the Baltimore and Ohio Railroads were interested in this line.[12] By autumn of 1860 freight cars equipped with wheels of so-called "compromise gauge" were moving all the way through from East St. Louis (then Illinois-town) to Bellaire, Ohio, the eastern terminal of the Ohio Central Railroad. This was accomplished by using the standard-gauge tracks of the Terre Haute and Alton and the Terre Haute and Richmond as far as Indianapolis and a series of 4 foot 10-inch roads from thence eastward.[13] Goods could be sent via this route all the way from St. Louis to Baltimore, but they had to be transshipped across the Ohio River to Wheeling. A second feeder line from the west, the Marietta and Cincinnati, served the Baltimore and Ohio. It provided the most direct route from Cincinnati to the Atlantic Coast. Although the Marietta and Cincinnati, like the Baltimore and Ohio, was of standard gauge, a break of bulk was necessary because the Ohio River had not yet been bridged at Parkersburg.[14]

Outside pressures then, in the form of the New York Central, the Pennsylvania, and the Baltimore and Ohio, operated to integrate the rail networks of Ohio and Indiana. All three of these eastern roads were standard gauge and, although they did not succeed immediately in changing over the tracks of their midwest allies to their own gauge, at least they did not add further to the complexity of the gauge pattern. Unfortunately, the same cannot be said for the Erie influence. Financial interests, allied with the Erie Railroad, completed in 1864 a line with a 6-foot gauge which angled across Ohio and connected the Erie with the broad-gauge Ohio and Mississippi at Cincinnati. In this one instance, outside influence further complicated the railroad map of Ohio at a time when sentiment was soon to favor a uniform gauge.

Throughout the other midwestern states, both local and outside factors operated in a way very similar to that just described for Ohio and Indiana. Outside promotion and financing played a major role in the newer states from the very beginning of the railroad era and the extent of their influence is reflected in the very wide adoption of the standard gauge. Attention will be confined here to one important instance in which commercial rivalry tended to retard the completion of the railroad net in this area.[15]

The commercial rivalry between St. Louis and Chicago somewhat resembled that between Philadelphia and New York. For decades St. Louis merchants had dominated the rich trade of the upper Mississippi and the Missouri region, but in the early fifties the merchants of Chicago emerged as serious rivals for this commerce. Railroad lines from Chicago were built north, west and south into rich lumber and farming areas; connections were made with railroads entering from the east; radiating lines reached one after another of the Mississippi River ports north of St. Louis and began to syphon away a portion of the down-river trade.[16] The Illinois Central Railroad, built southward to the Ohio River at Cairo, also threatened to develop a north-south commerce which would completely by-pass St. Louis.

To meet the threat of Chicago interests to a trade which they regarded as their own, the businessmen of St. Louis adopted two expedients. First, they gave their support to the construction of a railroad line from the east bank of the Mississippi opposite St. Louis, across southern Illinois and Indiana to Cincinnati. The question of bridging the Mississippi River at St. Louis does not seem to have been seriously considered at the time. The great cost and the difficulty of spanning the wide river at this point doubtless account for this, although the opposition of St. Louis steamboat interests may well have been a factor. At any rate, business leaders in St. Louis allied themselves with the merchants and land speculators of southern Illinois to promote the construction of railroad lines across the southern part of that state. In the ensuing struggle in the Illinois legislature over the chartering of cross-state railroads, Chicago interests, supported by Alton and other up-river rivals of St. Louis, opposed the proposal. But the legislative battle was won by the St. Louis interests and their allies in southern Illinois, and the result of the opposition was merely to delay temporarily the securing of a charter for the Ohio and Mississippi Railroad.[17] This line gave St. Louis a rail route to the east, although one which was handicapped both by its unusual gauge and by the lack of a bridge across the Mississippi.[18]

Further to thwart the Chicago bid for the trade of the Mississippi valley, the St. Louis Chamber of Commerce, representing the closely allied trading and steamboat interests of the city, strove persistently to prevent the construction of a railroad bridge across the Mississippi between Iowa and Illinois. Even after a bridge had been completed at Rock Island in 1856, St. Louis merchants vigorously but unsuccessfully sought its removal through court action.[19] The bitterness of this controversy is illustrated by an incident which took place at Chicago in 1860, when an attorney for the St. Louis Chamber of Commerce was arrested, thrown into jail, and charged with conspiring to burn the Rock Island Bridge. He was later acquitted.[20] A second bridge over the Mississippi was not completed until 1865. Apparently the persistent attacks by the St. Louis Chamber of Commerce upon the legality of the first bridge served as a temporary deterrent to the construction of others.[21]

THE BEGINNINGS OF A RAIL NETWORK IN THE SOUTH

Railroad construction in the southern states had gone forward with great rapidity in the decade of the fifties. Nevertheless, the southern network was less developed in 1861 than that in any other area east of the Mississippi. It was most complete in the seaboard states from Virginia to Georgia where population was densest and where most of the earliest construction had taken place. Railroad lines fanned out into the back country from the principal port or ports of each state, a pattern dictated by commercial considerations as well as by the difficulty of bridging arms of the sea and the broad estuaries of the rivers. North-south transportation over appreciable distances continued to depend chiefly on coastwise vessels. Interconnections among the state-oriented railroad systems were so inadequate that most interstate rail traffic had to move by indirect and roundabout routes.

Commercial interests in the leading southern ports strongly influenced the original railroad pattern. This is well illustrated in the building of the Charleston and Hamburg, the earliest important railroad in the South and one of the first in the country. Promoted by the Charleston Chamber of Commerce, this line was designed primarily to divert the rich trade of the Savannah River from Savannah to Charleston. A report of a committee of the Charleston Chamber of Commerce urging the construction of this road typifies the spirit of urban rivalry:

Charleston will and *must* be the great commercial mart of the surrounding states. No local jealousies can interrupt her march to wealth. No rival competition impede her progress to her 'Destined Elevation,' if her citizens are but faithful to *their own interest* and seize with a becoming energy those advantages which *providence* has placed at their disposal, and cultivate those vast resources of trade which lay invitingly within their reach.[22]

The southern seaboard state systems made through connections to the west by only two rail routes. One led to the southwest across Virginia and through Knoxville, Tennessee; the other proceeded to the northwest from Charleston and Savannah by way of Atlanta. These lines converged at Chattanooga, whence the Memphis and Charleston Railroad provided a through route to Memphis on the Mississippi River and afforded connections with most of the north-south railroads in this area. A second east-west route leading from Atlanta through Montgomery and Selma to Vicksburg on the Mississippi was only partly completed in 1861.

In Kentucky, Tennessee, Alabama, and Mississippi the chief railroad building effort had been directed toward completing north-south lines.[23] Here, as in the Old Northwest, mercantile groups strove not so much to erect exclusive systems as to construct roads which would connect their own city with distant markets. Thus, the two leading gulf cities, New Orleans and Mobile, sponsored rival lines which extended northward through Mississippi to make connections with the roads of Tennessee and Kentucky.[24] Louisville, the most aggressive of the Kentucky cities, reached southward through Bowling Green to complete connections not only with these roads but, via Chattanooga, with Atlanta, Savannah, and Charleston.

Elsewhere in the South the railroad era was just beginning in 1861, and only fragments of construction appear on the map. Florida had nearly completed two cross state lines, but these had no out-of-state connections. West of the Mississippi a rash of unconnected rail lines appears on the map, but only in the vicinity of Houston, Texas, are the beginnings of the network which was to develop after the war even suggested.

Some of the striking discontinuities of the southern railroad system which appear on the map are explainable by the newness of railroad development and were not deliberately created by any interest group. These hindrances to the movement of traffic were being eliminated as rapidly as capital became available and construction difficulties overcome. For example, the remaining gaps in the east-west route between Vicksburg and Atlanta and also the short gap between Corinth, Mississippi, and Jackson, Tennessee, were on the way to being closed when the war broke out in 1861.

On the other hand, several of the breaks in the southern railroad net resulted from commercial rivalries. The failure to connect the Florida railroads with those of Georgia prior to the war was in part because of the fear of Florida business interests that the trade of their state might be monopolized by Savannah instead of benefiting their own ports.[25] Again, a continuous line southward through the piedmont region of North Carolina was broken by the lack of a railroad between Greensboro, North Carolina, and Danville, Virginia. The need of a connection permitting through traffic to Richmond had long been recognized, but commercial interests in North Carolina, especially those at such port cities as New Bern and Wilmington, defeated all attempts to obtain a charter for such a road from the North Carolina legislature until Civil War needs made its construction imperative. The fear was that the trade from interior North Carolina would be diverted to Richmond and thus away from the state's own seaports.[26]

GAUGE DIFFERENCES IN THE SOUTH

Although a width of 4 feet 6 inches had been originally advised for the Charleston and Hamburg Railroad, Horatio Allen, who became chief engineer of the road in September 1829, recommended a 5-foot gauge on the basis of engineering considerations.[27] As will be seen from Map III, the decision to adopt this gauge greatly influenced railroad construction throughout most of the South. Georgia, South Carolina, and Tennessee railroads adopted it exclusively, and it was the predominant gauge in Kentucky, Mississippi, and Alabama. So far as gauge was concerned, rolling stock could be moved all the way from such Atlantic ports as Norfolk, Charleston, and Savannah to Louisville, Memphis, and New Orleans.

Nevertheless, a glance at the map will show that the South as a whole was bedeviled by serious gauge variations. A number of Virginia railroads were standard gauge, as were most of those of North Carolina. Kentucky, Mississippi, Louisiana, and Texas had short lines of this gauge. In Mississippi, the line leading eastward from Vicksburg had the distinction, unique for the South, of having a 4 foot 10-inch gauge.[28] Finally, it will be seen from the map of the Southern railroads that most of the track in the South west of the Mississippi was built to a 5 foot 6-inch width.

For the most part these gauge variations appear to reflect merely individual differences in judgment and a failure to appreciate the future of the railroad as a means for the long-distance transportation of freight and passengers. The adoption of the standard gauge in the border states is not surprising in view of the prevalence of this gauge to the north. But the building of roads to gauges other than that of 5 feet in Alabama and Mississippi seems logically incomprehensible. Nor is it clear from the available records why most of the Southern roads west of the Mississippi selected a width of 5 feet 6 inches.

To return to the East, the gauge pattern in North Carolina was more deliberately determined. Citizens of that state, especially those in the seaboard counties, had long resented the tendency of their commerce to flow south to Charleston or north to Petersburg, Richmond, and Portsmouth rather than to North Carolina's own inferior seaports. The coming of the railroad seemed to many North Carolina businessmen a real opportunity to correct this situation, and an early convention, held at Raleigh in 1833, adopted a resolution declaring that the state should utilize its resources "in creating and improving markets within her own limits" by the construction of railroads.[29] The tracks of the first railroad in the state, the Wilmington and Raleigh, were standard gauge, and though most of the roads in southern Virginia and all in South Carolina were to have a width of 5 feet, the state of North Carolina adhered persistently to its own gauge.

There was opposition, but the citizens of the coastal counties, and especially the merchants of such ports as Wilmington, New Bern, and Morehead City, were consistently successful in securing legislation requiring the roads of the state, with only two minor exceptions, to be standard gauge. They not only prevented a rail connection between Greensboro and Danville, Virginia, until forced by war needs to accede to the building of one, but also when the Piedmont Railroad was constructed for this purpose, they prevailed upon the legislature to require that it be standard gauge, despite its connection at Danville with the 5-foot gauge of the Richmond and Danville. Military necessity finally forced the legislature of North Carolina to approve changing the gauge to 5 feet, but the act by which this change was authorized carefully provided that the

44

gauge would have to be changed back to standard width within six months after the close of the war.[30]

Not apparent on the map, but at least as serious a barrier as gauge differences to through railroad traffic in the South, were the gaps in the railroad network in many southern cities. Sometimes these gaps accompanied gauge differences. At Montgomery, Alabama, through shipment was impeded not only because one railroad was standard gauge and the other 5 foot, but also because their terminals were separated by several city blocks.[31] Serious problems also arose in other river and seaport cities of the South Atlantic States where merchants in rival centers sought to build exclusive commercial empires.

When railroads were first built in these states, they were looked upon primarily as vehicles for trade with the nearby back country. They furnished an avenue of commerce to, not through, the port city. Their noise, the smoke, and the fire hazard of sparks showering from their wood-burning engines were unwelcome on the city streets, and consequently the early railroads to these port towns often had their terminals at the outskirts. Frequently, they made no connection with other rail lines leaving the city, nor did they extend to the waterfront where goods could be transferred directly from freight cars to barges or sailing vessels.

As the rail net spread in the fifties and with both freight and passenger traffic greatly increased, the need to permit the railroads to traverse the streets of the port cities became apparent. Spark arresters attached to the smokestacks of locomotives reduced the danger of fires, and the advantages of bringing the railroads into the commercial sections and down to the wharves influenced most towns to permit the practice. Nevertheless, in the chief river and seaport cities of the South Atlantic States the railroads were not permitted to make the actual connections which would permit an exchange of rolling stock or facilitate transfer of freight from one line to another.

This restriction was enforced by local business groups. Their interests were twofold: first, tavern keepers, teamsters, porters, forwarding agents, retail merchants, and others developed a vested interest in the transfer business which was dependent upon preserving a gap in the railroad line; second, the wholesale merchants wished to increase the business of their ports both for importing and exporting. As in the case of the merchants of Philadelphia, the Southern business groups did not wish their cities to become way stations with freight and passengers merely passing through. The reasoning was quite similar to that of merchants who, until fairly late in the automobile age, objected to the construction of highways which would by-pass the business districts of towns along a main road.

In contrast, the leading railroad centers in the South Atlantic States which were located inland and not on important waterways formed genuine junction points where rail lines were connected and rolling stock was shifted from one line to another. Burkesville, Virginia, and Columbia, South Carolina, for example, were important junctions permitting through movement of freight, as were such important inland Georgia cities as Macon and Atlanta.

The terminal of the Central of Georgia Railroad was on the opposite side of Savannah from that of the Savannah, Albany and Gulf Railroad.[32] Only after prolonged opposition was the South Carolina Railroad Company granted the privilege of building a bridge over the Savannah River and making a connection with the Georgia Railroad. Local commercial interests prevented the Augusta and Savannah line from forming a junction with other railroads entering the city.[33] The Ashley River separated the tracks of the Charleston and Savannah Railroad at Charleston from those of the two other railroads entering the city, and at Wilmington, North Carolina, the Cape Fear River as well as a gauge difference blocked through rail movement.[34]

The map shows a series of standard-gauge railroads leading north from Wilmington to Aquia Creek on the Potomac River. On this route lay two port cities, Petersburg and Richmond. In both of these cities local interests prevented the union of railroad lines, a position which was supported by an act of the Virginia legislature permitting cities to forbid railroad companies to use their streets. Four railroads entered Petersburg from south of the Appomattox River. None of these made connections with each other and, more important still, they were all separated by the river from the Richmond and Petersburg Railroad which terminated at Pocahontas opposite Petersburg. Although railroad interests sought to close these gaps, only the pressure of the Civil War was sufficient to over-

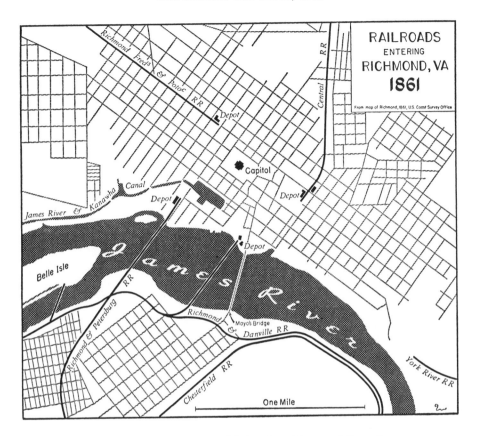

come the "great repugnance . . . felt by the citizens of Petersburg to any connection between the roads in question by means of which produce and merchandise would pass through Petersburg to and from Richmond." [35]

The situation at Richmond was closely parallel. None of the three railroads entering Richmond north of the James River made connections with each other or with the three railroads entering from the south, despite the fact that all but the Raleigh and Danville were standard gauge. The local opposition to through connections was so bitter here that when connections were forced because of the Civil War they were allowed with the provision that such links could be used for military purposes only.[36]

Finally, not only were southern railroads largely without internal in-

47

tegration, but they were also completely without direct rail connections with any other part of the nation. The lack of bridges over the Mississippi proved a barrier to the West as the unbridged Ohio River did to the North. And in northern Virginia, where gauges were the same as in Maryland, there was not a single direct connection with northern railroads, for at Alexandria and Aquia Creek the only means of transferring either goods or passengers was by steamboat.

VI

THE TREND TOWARD
INTEGRATION, 1861–1870

During the pre-railroad age in America western store-keepers made semiannual visits to the cities of the East, bought supplies for the coming season, and personally supervised the shipment of their goods to their stores in the interior. For example, a merchant from one of the small settlements in Michigan, purchasing his stock in Albany in 1825, arranged first for its shipment via the Erie Canal to Buffalo. At Buffalo he supervised its transfer to a lake boat on which he took passage to Detroit. At Detroit he arranged for transshipment to his own or hired wagons which finally carried his new stock to his place of business.

If a western merchant was unable to make his regular trip to the East, he had the alternative of sending a partner or other trustworthy substitute or of arranging with agents to act for him. Usually these agents were acquaintances in the cities in which he made his purchases and at the transfer points along the route by which his goods were sent to the West. The shipment of the Michigan merchant, had he been unable to accompany it himself, would doubtless have been consigned to an acquaintance in Buffalo, who would have gone down to the canal, collected the consignment, and had it delivered to a lake boat, after having bargained with the captain as to the charges. Another acquaintance of the merchant would have supervised the transshipment at Detroit.[1]

Early in the history of the westward movement, transfer or forwarding agents appeared at the principal points of transshipment, chiefly in re-

49

sponse to the needs of western shippers who were unable to accompany their produce to market. At least some of these were commission merchants who received consignments, forwarded the produce to market, and arranged for its sale.

The advent of the railroad effected no immediate change in the shipping pattern of internal America. Far from introducing through shipment, the early railways created additional obstacles to the free flow of traffic. Those arising from differences in gauge are merely the most obvious. There were many others, for the same limited view on the function of the railways which had led to the deliberate construction of roads of varying gauges also affected early railroad management. Thus, in the beginning, neither physical nor institutional means were provided for interline exchange. Each short railroad operated without any attempt to coordinate its services with those of other companies unless they were built specifically as allied extensions. Train schedules were drawn up with little attention to what adjoining lines might do. Neither the passenger nor freight cars of a company operated beyond the limits of the company's own tracks.

This latter state of affairs persisted much longer than is generally believed. In 1847, after the Hudson River had been bridged at Troy and when Boston for some years had been engaged in a grim struggle with the port of New York for the trade of the West, the Boston and Worcester and the Western Railroad, both Boston controlled, were not as yet interchanging cars with roads of the same gauge west of the Hudson.[2] Noting the disadvantages resulting from the unwillingness of railroads to exchange rolling stock even when of the same gauge, George Dartnell, writing in 1858, strongly advocated the establishment of a railroad clearing house. He writes in urging this proposal:

It would save many unnecessary transhipments, as such would only be required where there was a break of gauge; cars would invariably run through when fully laden, and be loaded on their return, either for a part or for the whole distance; the companies to whom they belonged receiving payment by a mileage toll for the distance traveled loaded; they would also be entitled to demurrage for additional time occupied in transit.

The many transhipments of freight are known to be the chief cause of delays, overcharges, and damages, besides adding greatly to the working expenses in labor and clerk-hire, and requiring large and costly accommodations for the performance of the service; the expense of an ordinary transhipment is not less than 25 cents per ton, and the delay but little under 24 hours, if any.

There is no reason why the running of cars through, should increase the mileage of "Empties," as foreign cars might be loaded from point to point, so long as they were not taken off the line of route by which they were received.

The interchange of passenger and freight cars under the present system is not only exceedingly limited, but is believed to be generally very unsatisfactory; and there can be but little doubt that if it were made usual with roads having the same gauge, it would tend to increase through traffic by railroads, to give greater confidence and satisfaction to the public, and to add to the revenues of the companies interested.[3]

In the course of the Senate debates in February 1863 on the question of the gauge of the first transcontinental railroad, the statement was made that the running of "strange" cars over their roads was something that good railroad managers would not permit.

It is something that ought never to be required, and never can be required if the rolling stock of the company is sufficient for its business. It is an advantage to the road itself as an independent road that it is not to be interrupted by other roads running into it or disturbing its own rolling stock. . . . They can better afford to break gauge and pay the expenses themselves.[4]

This, to be sure, was the argument of a senator who advocated a break of gauge at the Missouri River, but even his most articulate opponent had to admit that railroads frequently transshipped even where no break of gauge occurred as "a matter of convenience in keeping certain running stock on short lines of road, so as not to commingle the various interests. . . ."[5] In 1866 passengers on at least some of the trains running on the broad-gauge route between New York and St. Louis were forced to transfer at Cincinnati, not because of any physical obstacle but because the Ohio and Mississippi Railroad, which formed the link between Cincinnati and St. Louis, refused to let its cars leave its own line.[6] Summarizing the situation at the close of the Civil War, S. Morton Peto, who traveled widely in the United States, wrote: "Scarcely any attempts are made to render the working of lines convenient to travellers by working the trains of one company in conjunction with another. . . ."[7]

Matching the conservatism of railroad management was the long-continued parochialism of the cities. To local merchants it seemed clear that the uninterrupted movement of freight and passengers through their municipality contributed to the prosperity of a rival city where a trackage break occurred. Moreover, a forced transfer of through freight led to the development of forwarding companies and created jobs for the city's workers. The "Erie War" of 1855–56 was simply the most spectacular result of attempts to interfere with the vested interests that grew up wherever transshipment was necessary.[8] In denying, during the course of the debates referred to in the preceding paragraph, that he was influenced by local interests in advocating that the gauge of the Pacific Railroad match that of the Iowa lines, Senator James B. Grimes of Iowa explained:

. . . if I was controlled by any local interests, I should be in favor of the break of gauge, because wherever there is a break in the gauge there is always a large amount of business to be done, and a town immediately springs up around that place; but I trust that I look at the question in a national point of view. . . .[9]

As late as the summer of 1871 the city of Louisville extended "certain desirable privileges" to the Louisville, Cincinnati and Lexington Railroad, a road of 5-foot gauge on the south side of the Ohio, in consideration of the road's changing its gauge to 4 feet 9 inches and thus compelling transfers to be made in Louisville which might otherwise be made in Cincinnati.[10]

FACTORS ENCOURAGING RAILWAY INTEGRATION

Despite continued local efforts to profit by the differences in gauge and breaks in track, by the decade of the 1860's there were signs of a new order for America's railroads. Satisfying as such traffic breaks might be to local interests, they placed a heavy tax on through freight. As this class of freight became more important, the need to eliminate physical obstacles became imperative, and uniformity of gauge was forced upon the railroads of the United States and Canada.

By the outbreak of the Civil War, the very eastern merchants who had been responsible for the early pattern of railway development in America and who were not as yet prepared to give up any real or imagined advantages arising from trackage breaks in their own cities were complaining of the costs of transfers on the lines over which they shipped and of the overcharges of forwarding agents. In 1863 it was estimated that a single transshipment cost an average of seven cents a ton. The Boston Board of Trade maintained in 1866 that such costs on the roads between their city and Chicago amounted to $500,000 a year.[11]

Agitation on the part of the seaboard merchants for the more efficient handling of through freight coincided with other developments of the 1860's which led to substantial advances toward an integrated railroad network. One of these was the Civil War, which brought with it the necessity of large-scale movement of troops and supplies. Another was the decision of Congress that the newly chartered Pacific Railroad should be of standard gauge, thus assuring that the railway system west of the Missouri River would develop as part of the nation's system, not as a separate system. A third significant development of this period affecting the railroad pattern was the growth of the grain trade from the West.

EFFECT OF THE CIVIL WAR

Technological and institutional innovations of the war years in response to military needs resulted for some areas of the country in a breakdown of the carefully isolated railway systems of the rival commercial interests.[12] In the South, for instance, the railroads entering Richmond were joined by tracks laid through the streets. This was in direct response to military needs and over the opposition of local interests. The roads entering Petersburg were also joined, and the gap was finally closed between Greensboro, North Carolina, and Danville, Virginia.[13] Legislatures sometimes carefully stipulated that tracks laid for military purposes were to be removed after the war. But when the war was over and the badly damaged railroads of the South were rebuilt, partly with Northern and European capital, it was possible to ignore local pressures.

In the North, the war years saw the inauguration of through railroad service between New York and Washington. With the greatly increased need for fast and efficient rail service along the eastern seaboard, the persistence of Philadelphia interests in preventing rail connections at that city became intolerable. A *New York Times* editorial declared no "railroad in the world is in so shameless a condition of inefficiency and discomfort as that between New York and Washington,"[14] and, referring to the earlier gauge dispute at Erie, stated that: "Philadelphia . . . has not entirely outgrown the village peevishness manifested at Erie."[15]

Beginning in 1862 a car ferry crossing the Delaware River at Camden connected the Camden and Amboy and the Philadelphia, Wilmington and Baltimore Railroads. The ferry permitted some direct movement of rolling stock, but not very effectively, for the service was inadequate and the gauge difference of 1½ inches between the two roads caused difficulties.[16] Finally, in 1863, the railroads secured through service from north to south by connections around Philadelphia, and the need for changing cars in that city was eliminated. The president and directors of the Philadelphia, Wilmington and Baltimore Railroad stated in their report of that year to the stockholders that "this most desirable object" (the elimination of the traffic break in the City of Brotherly Love) had been achieved "by using a part of . . . The Philadelphia and Reading, the Junction, the Pennsylvania Central, and the West Chester." "This arrangement . . . though by no means perfect," the report continued, "thus far gives great satisfaction to the traveling public." [17] It also gave great satisfaction to the railroad managements concerned as well as to the New York, Baltimore, and Washington merchants who had been demanding such through service for some time.[18]

Throughout the war, efforts to improve the Northern trunkline systems went forward. Built during this period was the Atlantic and Great Western, a road of 6-foot gauge which connected with the Erie at Salamanca, New York, and with the Cincinnati, Hamilton and Dayton at Dayton, Ohio. In 1864 the latter road completed a "straddle track" — a broad-gauge track placed outside its 4-foot 10-inch rails — in order to accommodate the cars of the Erie and the Atlantic and Great Western. At Cincinnati, the Cincinnati, Hamilton and Dayton connected with the 6-foot Ohio and Mississippi, thus completing a broad-gauge line without a single physical obstacle between the eastern seaboard and the Mississippi River opposite St. Louis.[19] By the end of 1865 the 5-foot 6-inch Great Western of Canada, which formed the connecting link between the New York Central and the Michigan Central railroads (both standard-gauge roads), was laying a third rail for the future accommodation of standard-gauge cars.[20]

In reporting these improvements the Boston Board of Trade commented:

. . . in New York . . . the advantages of uniform gauge are well understood. . . . this process of assimilation in gauge on the Central and Western lines is constantly going forward; and whatever interested parties may say to the contrary, breaking bulk will soon come to be no more tolerated in a freight car when once loaded at the West with produce destined to the sea-board, than it would be in a canal boat similarly laden.

54

It becomes the people of Boston then, to look carefully to their connections with the West.[21]

The determination of eastern interests not to tolerate new artificially imposed barriers to the free flow of traffic is evident from the circumstances surrounding the fixing of the gauge of the Pacific Railroad. It is sometimes assumed that American railroads have a standard gauge of 4 feet 8½ inches because that gauge was chosen by Congress for the first transcontinental line, and it is thought that this decision forced conformity upon connecting roads and subsequently upon all roads. An examination of the Senate debates on the matter,[22] however, leads to the inescapable conclusion that the gauge of the Union Pacific–Central Pacific was set at 4 feet 8½ inches largely because this measurement already predominated in the country. In other words, standard gauge had been determined for America before Congress acted on the gauge of the Pacific Railroad.

The first Pacific Railroad Act of July 1, 1862, left the decision concerning the gauge of the transcontinental line to President Lincon. Lincoln, after consulting engineers and railroad men through the Department of the Interior, and after discussing the matter with his full cabinet, set the gauge at five feet,[23] which was the gauge of the California railroads. The railroad interests of the East and Midwest, already largely committed to standard gauge, resolved not to accept the president's decision but to use the overwhelming power of their sections in Congress to set it aside. Accordingly, in January 1863, James Harlan, senator from Iowa, introduced into the Senate a bill to establish the gauge of the Pacific Railroad at 4 feet 8½ inches.[24]

The debates which ensued are revealing not only of sectional interests but also of the state of opinion concerning the desirability and the practicability of a uniform railroad gauge for the entire country. Proponents of the bill leaned heavily in their arguments on the advantages of interline exchange, especially in times of war — advantages which would be lost if the gauge of the Pacific Railroad were allowed to stand at five feet. They pointed to the preponderance of the standard gauge throughout the North and the Middle West (an estimated 20,567 miles to 1,199 miles of roads of other gauge), and to the large investments which had been made in the construction of those roads ($849,000,000 to $60,000,000 for all other lines). Not a road in the Northwest, they maintained, would be able to exchange equipment with the transcontinental line, if the gauge of that line were five feet.

Opponents of the bill scoffed at the idea of sending cars, either passenger or freight, over long distances without change. Transshipment, they said, was necessary for purposes of cleanliness and safety. Cars should be aired and merchandise examined at regular intervals. Moreover, there were limits to the distance which both locomotives and cars could be safely run without allowing the equipment to cool. One senator was of the opinion that since the Missouri River could probably never be bridged, it was a matter of no importance whether the gauge of the Pacific Railroad was in conformity with that of the connecting roads to the east. Therefore he urged that the President's choice of gauge be allowed to stand.

When the vote on Senator Harlan's bill providing for standard gauge was taken, Eastern interests won an easy victory, the count being 23 to 9 in favor of the bill. The senators from California and Oregon were joined in dissent by only five senators from states east of the Missouri River.[25] The bill passed the House without debate and without a record vote.[26]

GROWTH OF THE GRAIN TRADE

When Eastern interests dictated a gauge of 4 feet 8½ inches for the first transcontinental railroad line, they were undoubtedly mindful of the traffic in grain which in the near future would flow from the area west of Omaha. For several generations after the first white men defied the barrier of the Appalachians, western produce had found its way to eastern markets via the Mississippi to New Orleans and from there by ocean vessels to Atlantic ports. By the outbreak of the Civil War, however, the western carrying trade had been almost completely reoriented, relatively direct east-west canal and railroad routes having replaced the old circuitous river and sea route.[27] Heavy or bulky products such as lead from the Galena mines or corn and wheat from the upper Mississippi Valley and the Old Northwest continued to move for the most part by water, chiefly via the Great Lakes, the Erie Canal, and the Hudson River.[28] Less weighty or bulky freight such as hides and animals was usually taken east by rail. The carrying trade in flour, an important item in internal commerce, was fairly evenly divided between water and land carriage, 365,000 barrels being shipped eastward by lake in 1859, and 307,000 barrels by railroad.[29]

Although grain moved from the West to the eastern seaboard chiefly by water, the railroads played an auxiliary role in the traffic. So long as the water route was open the railways were largely confined to hauling wheat and corn from the interior to a lake port and from Buffalo to internal markets, but after the close of navigation in the fall or early winter, surplus grain which had piled up in the lake cities was frequently sent all the way to market by rail. Despite the limited character of the railroads' role in the grain trade, beginning at least as early as 1860, the freight earnings of the eastern trunk lines and their connections began to reflect an increasing traffic from the West, some of it in grain. In September 1860 the *American Railway Review* noted that the superintendent of the New York Central had ordered all spare cars to Suspension Bridge and Buffalo. "The freight gathering at those places, destined for the Eastern market, is immense, and will require the entire rolling stock to send it forward." [30] During that same year shipments of grain to Philadelphia increased by 300,000 bushels, nearly all of the increase being in wheat. Some of it moved all the way from the West by rail, for according to the Philadelphia Board of Trade, the Pennsylvania Central and its connections were "provided with a complete equipment of cars for bringing grain in bulk from Chicago without transshipment." [31]

It was not that the rails at this date were taking business away from the water routes, but rather that the demand for shipping was so heavy that it strained all transportation facilities to capacity. Then came the Civil War and the cutting off of the southern market for western produce. This coincided with increased demands for such produce from the rapidly industrializing eastern United States and from a Europe plagued with poor harvests. The result was that in February 1865 it was stated on good authority that not more than two-thirds of the grain crop of the Northwest, with *all* the transportation then available, could reach an eastern market that year.[32]

In the period following the Civil War the railroads were to absorb an ever larger portion of the carrying trade in grain.[33] In adapting plant and services to this traffic as well as to the general increase in internal commerce, American railway management was to forge from the many small lines of the pre-war period a truly national, not to say international, railroad system.

57

VII

SOLVING THE GAUGE DIFFERENTIALS, 1861-1880

"COMPROMISE" AND SLIDING WHEELS; CAR HOISTS

Preceding chapters have shown that by the time Lincoln entered the White House regional rivalries had led to a degree of integration along railroad routes which were tributary to the commercial centers of the East. While attempting by means of trackage breaks and gauge differences to keep business from their rivals, the merchants of each place had worked for an unhindered flow of traffic over the ever-lengthening transportation lines radiating from their own city. The trend toward integration was accelerated by the events of the Civil War period, particularly by the growth of the trade from the West, but at the close of the war the railway pattern of the United States and Canada was still characterized by its disjointedness.

The task of railroad management over the next twenty-five years was to build an integrated network. This called for action on two levels: first, a struggle with the vested interests at transfer points, entailing a long-drawn-out battle between entrenched local businessmen and city fathers on the one hand and shippers and railroad interests on the other; and second, the solution of the technological problems involved in the process of integration. It is the purpose of this chapter to deal with the latter development.

The joining of the tracks of two or more railroads within a town or at junction points was simple so long as the roads were of the same gauge.

Where a difference of gauge existed the obvious and inevitable solution was to bring the gauges of the roads into conformity. This, however, was prohibitively expensive, for change of gauge involved not only the moving of the rails, but also the change-over of rolling stock. Few railroads could afford to pay the bill, but neither could they afford to surrender through traffic to other lines. The result was that a number of temporary expedients were devised which permitted interchange of equipment between lines of different gauge and eliminated the necessity of trans-shipment.

There were at least three such expedients. Most simple was the "compromise car" having wheels with 5-inch surfaces which permitted the car to run over tracks with a gauge as narrow as 4 feet 8½ inches and as broad as 4 feet 10 inches. Such cars were in use as early as 1860. By 1870 there were thousands of compromise cars in service,[1] although the wide wheels were frowned upon by careful railroad men, one of whom described the use of such wheels as "questionable, if not dangerous,"[2] for a number of accidents could be traced to the broad treads.

At best, cars with compromise wheels were limited to gauges no wider than 4 feet 10 inches, and were of no use as a means of interchanging traffic between roads of standard and of 5-foot or 6-foot gauge. Two other devices were developed to meet this situation. In 1863 the railroads experimented with cars having wheels designed to slide on their axles. These cars could be accommodated to both standard and broad gauge and could be easily shifted from one gauge to the other if at junction points the track widened or narrowed gradually. The wheels of the cars were loosened by means of a simple, hand-operated mechanism, the cars were run slowly onto the connecting track, and the wheels were then locked in the new position. In November 1863 a car of this description was run over the standard-gauge Eastern Railroad to Portland and from there over the Grand Trunk, a road of 5 foot 6-inch gauge, to Island Pond, where it was loaded with flour for Boston. The car reached Boston without mishap, having for a second time negotiated the transfer from a broad to a standard-gauge road. According to its inventor, Charles S. Tisdale, the car was a "perfect success," and had received the approval of the officers of the roads over which it had traveled. The commercial community of Boston, still jealous of Portland and resentful of the break of gauge at that city, took a deep interest in the new car, although they regarded any advantage arising from the use of cars with adjustable wheels as only a "mitigation" of the "evil" of diverse gauges.[3]

By the early 1870's the Grand Trunk and its connections were reported to have in operation as many as a thousand cars with sliding wheels. The cars failed to perform well in service, however, for as time went on the number of accidents in which they were involved increased alarmingly, either because the wheel fastenings were secured carelessly or because the fastenings worked loose in running. The result was that during 1873 and 1874 the Grand Trunk, at great expense, narrowed the gauge of its entire line — some 1300 miles of track — to standard width in order to conform to the gauge of its connections at Portland, St. John, Buffalo, and Detroit.[4]

More successful than sliding wheel cars were car hoists, usually referred to in their day as "elevating machines." The hoists were used at transfer points to lift the bodies of cars, either passenger or freight, while trucks of one gauge were exchanged for those of another, without it being necessary to unload the cars. By means of such a hoist the 6-foot Erie in the mid-1870's exchanged traffic with the standard-gauge Great Western of Canada.[5] At the same date there were at least two car hoists in operation along the Ohio, one at Cairo, Illinois, the other at Henderson, Kentucky, where the prevailing standard gauge of the North met the 5-foot gauge of the South.[6]

The hoist at Henderson was built to raise either one freight car or two passenger cars. It was constructed according to the screw principle and was powered by a small stationary steam engine. A car was hoisted in less than half a minute, while changing the trucks took not more than five or six minutes. A contemporary observer has left a description of the operation:

The trucks are shifted by means of two transverse tables, one at each end. These tables run upon tracks and carry the trucks to a siding. . . and bring back those of different gauge. . . . [By] this arrangement, when two cars of different gauges are changed at the same time, the trucks of one car are simply run forward under the body of the other. . . .[7]

According to Captain H. W. Tyler, a railway expert who was hired in 1874 by a group of English stockholders to make a survey of the plant and operations of the Erie, car hoists had not yet, at that date, been tried on a large scale. But Tyler had faith in their efficiency, suggesting that the Erie, if reluctant to assume the expense (estimated at $8,500,000) of changing the road's gauge from broad to standard, might invest in additional hoists to facilitate the movement of traffic between its road and roads of narrower gauge. In another context Tyler placed the cost of each such hoist at $3000.[8]

By 1880 elevating machines had become familiar sights to travelers in America. Early in the decade a foreign visitor reported steam hoists at Cincinnati, Ohio, and Lynchburg, Virginia, and described their operation in some detail.[9] By 1886 the Louisville and Nashville Railroad alone had such machines at nine different transfer points: Louisville, East Louisville, Rowland, Nortonville, and Henderson, Kentucky; Evansville, Indiana; Milan, Tennessee; Mobile, Alabama; and New Orleans, Louisiana.[10] "Each point of connection was a 'frontier' . . . between two 'foreign countries' . . . ."[11] The tracks at such junction points had three or four rails to accommodate the cars of different gauges, while "acres of extra trucks," some of one gauge, some of another, stood in the yards.[12]

"DOUBLE" GAUGES

Car hoists functioned efficiently enough so long as traffic was light. This accounts in part for their long use by the southern railroads. But where traffic was heavy, as on the trunk lines and their connections, the five or six minutes required to change the trucks of each car caused intolerable delays and tie-ups. Here car hoists had but slight, if any, retarding effect on the change to standard gauge. This statement is well illustrated by the experience of the Erie.

Senator Ira Harris of New York maintained as early as February 1863 that "men of capital engaged in the management of the Erie" were seriously considering taking up the road's rails and adopting the narrow (that is, standard) gauge for the sake of economy.[13] Ten years later, in announcing that an eventual change to standard gauge had been decided upon, the directors of the Erie reported to the stockholders:

Not only is this change demanded for the purpose of reducing working expenses, but because we cannot, so long as our gauge is not in conformity with that of our Western, Eastern and Southern connections, secure a large amount of traffic now offered to us, if we could receive and transport it without breaking bulk.[14]

In 1874, by which year the principal point of interchange between the Erie and its western connections had been transferred from Dunkirk to East Buffalo, the Company's yard for eastbound business at the latter place contained twenty tracks, altogether about fifteen miles long, "and . . . large transfer-sheds for changing goods between narrow and broad gauge cars." There was also a "Dodd's machine" for the hoisting of cars and the changing of trucks.[15] It will be remembered that Captain Tyler in his report to the English stockholders whom he represented suggested the installation of additional car hoists as a means of overcoming the disadvantages arising from the Erie's broad gauge. He also pointed out that the laying of a third rail for the accommodation of standard-gauge equipment was another possible alternative to the Erie's changing its gauge.[16]

During the three decades subsequent to 1860 a number of roads laid a third rail in order to accommodate equipment of a gauge other than their own. The case of the Great Western of Canada was noted in the preceding chapter. The Erie, as a matter of fact, had started to put down a third rail prior to June 1873, after attempts to make broad gauge connections with Chicago had come to nothing.[17] Managerial and financial difficulties, from which the Erie suffered chronically in the seventies, delayed the completion of the project until December 1878. After that date this line made unhindered connections with all the roads on which its foreign business originated, and was at last in a position to compete with the New York Central for through traffic from the lines both north and south of the Great Lakes.[18]

The management of a road seldom regarded a track of three rails as permanent. Sections of lines and junction railways which were designed for the indefinite accommodation of equipment of two different gauges usually had four rails in order that the weight of the rolling stock and consequently the wear on the rails might be evenly distributed. The laying of a third rail was more often than not but an intermediate step in the changing of a road's gauge to standard.[19] In this respect the advantages of a third rail were two: first, it allowed an immediate interchange of equipment with the road's connections while in no way interfering with the use of the road's old rolling stock on its own line; and second, it permitted a gradual changeover of the road's equipment to standard gauge, thus saving the company the expense of changing all its equipment at once.

Broad and standard-gauge cars and locomotives could be operated over a three-rail line with equal efficiency. On one road, at least, trains of mixed equipment were run. Shortly after the Great Western's third rail was completed in 1867, the general manager of the Blue Line, a fast freight line running over the road, reported: "The third rail from Windsor to Suspension Bridge, which enables the Great Western Railway to run their Broad Gauge Cars in the same train with 'Blue Line' or Narrow Gauge Cars, has . . . proved a perfect success." [20] Unfortunately the report is silent as to operational details. More usually trains operating over a road with three rails were made up of equipment of uniform gauge.[21]

The changeover of a road's rolling stock was begun as soon as the third rail was completed. Cars were adapted to the new gauge by changing the trucks. With the use of a steam hoist such as those in service at transfer points, the change could be made at the rate of ten cars an hour,[22] but the cost of new trucks was a considerable drain upon a company's resources. Conversion of motive power to a narrower gauge was so difficult that where there was a large difference between the old gauge and the new, such conversion was considered inexpedient.[23] These facts account for the long transitional period during which a number of roads operated with a third rail.

By 1880 there were perhaps 2800 miles of double gauge railroad in the United States. "A large proportion of the double gauges," the census of that year stated, "are formed by means of a third rail." Most roads of double gauge represented efforts to accommodate broad-gauge lines to standard-gauge equipment, or vice versa. But perhaps 400 miles of such road made possible the interchange of traffic between lines of standard gauge and of 3-foot or narrow gauge, of which approximately 5000 miles had been constructed during the "narrow gauge fever" of the 1870's.[24]

NARROW GAUGE RAILWAYS

At the very time that old established roads were changing from broad to standard gauge, a number of new roads were being built to a narrow, usually 3-foot, gauge. Roads of this gauge were unknown in the United States before 1870. Enthusiasm for them here, as in England, stemmed from a paper, "The Gauge for the 'Railways of the Future,'" read that year by Robert F. Fairlie at the British Railway Association's annual meeting.[25] The arguments of Fairlie and his followers, it must be admitted,

63

were plausible. A road of 3 foot 6-inch gauge, they claimed, was both cheaper to build and less expensive to maintain than a road of standard or broad gauge. A similar claim could be made for the construction and operation of narrow-gauge equipment. Moreover, it was pointed out, a narrow track was better adapted to mountainous regions, while it was only common sense to build a road designed for lighter equipment where traffic was light. Some proponents of the narrow gauge were even ready to defend the usefulness of their system in heavy traffic areas. Armed with statistics, they sought to prove that by simply increasing the number of cars and locomotives the same volume of freight might be moved by narrow-gauge as by standard or broad-gauge roads. Further, this could be done without excessive wear and tear on the right of way, for the lighter cars and locomotives would be easier on the rails.[26]

The subject of narrow-gauge railways is one of the most interesting ones now before the public [remarked the editor of the *Baltimore American* in the late spring of 1871], for if the plan succeeds as well here as it has done in Europe it will undoubtedly carry railroad facilities to many localities which would otherwise be deprived of them for years.[27]

The editor of the Boston *Commercial Bulletin* was of the opinion that narrow-gauge roads were especially adapted to the work of opening up the resources of new and sparsely settled regions, "where the topography of the country is mountainous, and the initial traffic to be secured is not sufficient to justify the outlay required for building a broad [that is, standard] gauge road." Also, narrow-gauge roads might be cheap feeders to the trunk lines.[28]

The entire railway world seemed to split into two factions over the merits of the narrow gauge, for the claims of its promoters did not go unchallenged. The battle was fought in the newspapers and the trade journals, at local, regional, and national meetings. The critics of the narrow-gauge mania were armed with their own figures which purported to show the real inefficiency of the narrow gauge. The most telling argument of this side, however, was concerned with the difficulties of interchanging traffic with roads of broader gauge. Here they could present contemporary examples of the inconveniences experienced at such transfer points as Dunkirk, Buffalo, and the towns along the Ohio and the Potomac Rivers. Since there was no refuting the evidence, the advocates of the narrow gauge were inclined to ignore the issue or to mark it as "practically of minor importance." [29] Some maintained that the costs of transfer would represent but a small fraction of the amount ultimately saved in construction, equipment, and maintenance.

The first great impetus given the narrow-gauge movement in the United States was the decision to adopt the 3-foot gauge made by the Denver and Rio Grande Railroad Company, which in the early 1870's was building its line in Colorado. Other new roads followed the example of the D. and R. G. By November 1874 it was reported that 1677 miles of narrow-gauge roads had been built in the Union, and that such roads were to be found in almost every state and territory, "but as a rule for short distances only." The Denver and Rio Grande, with "about 150 miles" of track, was the longest.[30] By January 1, 1878, the nation had 2862 miles of narrow-gauge railroad. About half of it was to be found in the lightly settled area west of the Mississippi, 350 miles of it in Colorado alone. East of the Mississippi, the greatest narrow-gauge mileages were in Ohio, which had 271 miles, Pennsylvania, which had 261 miles, and Illinois, which had 202 miles.[31] By 1880 the narrow-gauge trackage figure for the United States had climbed to the neighborhood of 5200, representing about 5 per cent of the total railroad trackage of the country.[32] In the single year 1882 some 2000 miles of narrow gauge track were laid.[33] This was the high point.

Before another year had passed, the *Railroad Gazette*, which had always been opposed editorially to the building of narrow-gauge roads, reported not without satisfaction that, although the narrow gauge still had many adherents, "the influence of this remarkable delusion has probably expended itself." [34] By the spring of 1884 the pioneer narrow-gauge line, the Denver and Rio Grande, had laid a third rail over the oldest part of its road, the section between Denver and Pueblo, for the accommodation of the standard-gauge equipment of its eastern connections.[35]

The narrow-gauge lines were but repeating the experience of the Erie and other broad-gauge roads in the northeastern United States and Canada. It could be argued that the costs of transshipment were insignificant when compared to the money saved in the construction and operation of narrow-gauge lines, but the shipper still thought of himself as paying the bill. Moreover, as Captain Tyler discovered in the case of the Erie in 1874, both travelers and shippers tended to shun roads on which breaks of gauge were known to exist.[36] Like the broad-gauge roads, narrow-gauge lines that were in competition for through traffic had to make arrangements for the accommodation of standard-gauge equipment or lose the business to standard-gauge lines. By the middle of the 1880's this hard fact had tempered the enthusiasm for narrow gauge.

VIII

THE FAST FREIGHT LINES, 1861-1890

BACKGROUND

The costs and inconveniences of transshipment had always weighed particularly heavily on the traffic from the West, its produce being both bulky and highly susceptible to loss and damage from frequent handling. In 1869 it cost 52¼ cents to transport a bushel of wheat from the Mississippi to New York, sending it by rail to Chicago and from there over the Great Lakes–Erie Canal route. Actual freight and toll charges amounted to only 40 cents; inspection and insurance absorbed another 1½ cents. Storage, handling, elevator charges, and commissions accounted for the remaining 10¾ cents.[1] Thus the cost of the services attendant upon transshipment equaled about 20 per cent of the total cost of shipping by this route.

The ability of the railroads to cut the costs and to eliminate the inconveniences of transshipment by offering through service was one factor in the phenomenal increase in the volume of grain moving east by rail in the period following the Civil War. Another factor was the ability of the roads to offer year-round service. In 1869 the directors of the Michigan Central Railroad remarked that "the transportation of grain in bulk to the seaboard has occurred during the past winter to *a very large* extent for the first time in the history of the railroads of the country. . . ."[2] Four years later the same authorities reported: "The grain of the country is now moved half the year, mainly by rail, and largely at all times."[3]

The Michigan Central directors gave entire credit for the increased grain traffic of the railroads to the fast freight lines,[4] organizations which had arisen in response to the need for through service and for large numbers of new freight cars. These nineteenth-century fast freight lines are to be distinguished from what are known as "fast freights" today, the latter being simply specially expedited, often regularly scheduled, trains which are given running preferences over ordinary "tonnage" freight in order to facilitate shipment, often of particular commodities. The original fast freight lines were independent of the railroads, owned their own cars, and operated over any number of roads. Their service was "fast" in that the cars of the line went through from their point of pick-up to their destination without breaking bulk, thus eliminating delays at transfer points.

Prior to this time, it is true, there had been some interchange of equipment between roads. As early as 1855, for instance, the Buffalo and Erie was regularly accepting the cars of western roads for transit over its line so that produce might go through to Buffalo without the necessity of handling.[5] But this was an enlightened attitude that was not shared by all roads. Moreover, differences in gauge continued to make transshipment necessary.

The advantage of the fast freight lines to the shipper was that they controlled their own cars which, when necessary, were equipped with "compromise" or adjustable wheels that could be accommodated to small differences in gauge and that could therefore be sent over most roads without the necessity of transshipping.[6] Where large differences in gauge made interline exchange impossible, the volume of business which the fast freight lines came to offer in many instances forced the management of deviant lines to make adjustments for the accommodation of the fast freight cars. The third rail which went into service on the Great Western of Canada in 1867, for instance, was laid to permit the passage of the cars of the Blue Line from the tracks of the New York Central at Suspension Bridge (Niagara) to those of the Michigan Central at Detroit.[7] An authority on the history of American railroads, writing at the end of the 1880's, was of the opinion that

only a very small proportion of the through-rail freight movements of the country would ever have been possible without the . . . freight lines, because it was mainly, and almost exclusively, through them, that the transfer of freight from one set of cars to another set of cars, at the connecting point between two lines, was abolished. . . .[8]

EARLY FAST FREIGHT LINES

The earliest fast freight lines predate the Civil War. Kasson's Dispatch, a line operating over the New York Central and its connections and usually cited as the first of them, seems to have appeared about 1855 or 1856. One authority states that this line later "merged into the Merchants' Dispatch."[9] The latter line was an outgrowth of the American Express Company and was in operation at least as early as January, 1856, when it was "guaranteeing the delivery of goods at Chicago in twelve days, at the uniform price of $2.10 a hundred for all classes."[10] The Great Western Dispatch, operating over the Erie Railway and its connections, dated from 1857. Yet another fast freight line, the Western Insurance and Transportation Company (known later as the Star Union Line), operating over the Pennsylvania and its connections, was chartered before the war, although it was not organized until 1864.[11] The other fast freight lines, exceeding perhaps forty in number, belong to the post-war period.

Since the original fast freight lines (later called "noncoöperative" lines) were independent stock companies, it might properly be asked what railway management stood to gain by interposing an outside organization between itself and the shipper. There are two answers to this. First, the demand for the large number of new freight cars that were needed to carry the increased western business came at a time when the unstable financial condition of many railroads made it impossible for the roads themselves to purchase cars in quantity. The alternative to some such device as the freight lines was to let business go begging. Secondly, the promoters and stockholders of the freight lines were often the officers of the railroads over which the lines operated. In their role as officers of the roads these men were in a position to give extremely favorable terms to the freight lines, thus increasing their own earnings as stockholders in the fast freights at the sacrifice of the earnings of the railroads' stockholders.

A notable example of such dualism and its consequences was found in New England, where in the 1870's the stocks of the fast freight lines operating over the Central Vermont, the Vermont and Canada, the Grand Trunk, the Boston and Lowell, and other railways were owned mainly by the officers of the railroad companies. The fact that the freight lines were paying ten to twelve per cent to their stockholders while the Vermont Central was in the hands of a receiver might well have set the public to questioning such close community of interests. A legislative inquiry elicited the information that not only were the cars of the freight lines given running privileges over the Vermont Central's own cars but also that a number of freight-line cars had been built in the railroad's shops and sold to the freight lines at scarcely more than cost.[12]

A committee of the United States Senate which investigated the fast freight lines in 1874 reported:

> The inducements on the part of railway companies to contract with such [fast freight] companies are ostensibly to secure the large aggregate of traffic they claim to control, but in a great many cases a division of profits between the officers of the railway company and the persons entering into these contracts is effected by a judicious distribution of their stock.[13]

The contracts of the fast freight lines with the railroads varied, but in the early years, at least, they usually provided that the freight lines pay the roads a certain flat rate per car, the rate being based on an estimated average of the tariff received from a like amount of freight of all classes in the general traffic of the road. In a number of cases the rate per car was based on a fixed tonnage that was somewhat less than the car's capacity. In turn, the railroads paid the freight lines a mileage rate ranging from $1\frac{1}{2}$ cents to 3 cents a mile for the use of the line's cars.[14]

Such contracts left room for a number of abuses. First, inasmuch as the profit of the freight lines was represented by the difference between the amount the lines collected from shippers and the amount they paid the railroads, it was to the advantage of the lines to solicit and to give preference to the higher classes of freight, leaving any lower-class freight which could not be accommodated in the through cars for the railroads to carry in their own cars. The consequence was that while the freight lines grew prosperous through carrying higher-class freight the railroads failed to break even on the only traffic left to them. Moreover, the freight lines, paying, as they were, a flat rate per car and that rate based on something less than the car's capacity, were tempted not only to load to capacity, but to overload — a practice that enhanced the freight company's earnings, but also increased wear and tear on track and roadbed.[15]

As a result of criticism of these practices, a number of the freight lines made new contracts with the railroads. According to the terms of the new contracts, the lines were simply paid by the roads for the use of their cars and for their services in soliciting freight. On the western roads payment was usually on a mileage basis, but in the East a percentage of the tariff collected by the railroads was generally paid the freight lines, which, consequently, came to be known as "commission" lines.[16] To quote one authority, "The effect of the second plan was, in a great many cases, as bad as that of the first," for, because of the community of interests between railroad management and the stockholders in the freight lines, new ways of siphoning profits from the railroads to the freight lines were soon discovered.[17]

COÖPERATIVE FAST FREIGHT LINES

Beginning in the late 1860's the demand for reform in the organization and management of the fast freight lines led to the development of what were known as "coöperative" freight lines. The first of these was the Red Line which dated from 1866 and ran between Chicago in the west and New York and Boston in the east, via Toledo, Buffalo and Albany. The second coöperative line to go into operation was the Blue Line which opened for business on January 1, 1867; it served the same terminals as the Red Line but its route lay north of the Great Lakes.[18]

The coöperative lines differed from the original fast freight lines in that they were not separate corporations but merely administrative organizations under the authority of the railroad companies coöperating in the line. While the cars of the line were operated in a pool, they were owned individually by the coöperating railroads. For instance, the ownership of the 96 cars of the Green Line, the principal fast freight line in the South, at the time of its organization in 1868 was divided as follows: Louisville and Nashville, 25; Nashville and Northwestern, 12; Nashville, Chattanooga and St. Louis, 31; Western and Atlantic, 28.[19] By 1881 nineteen southern roads were associated in the Green Line, which then controlled 3404 cars. Over 1000 were the property of the Nashville, Chattanooga and St. Louis. One road, the Northeastern Georgia, contributed as few as 2 cars to the line.[20] The same system prevailed on the fast freight lines north of the Ohio and Potomac: the quotas of cars furnished the lines by the roads were determined according to the length of the individual road or according to the amount of revenue the road derived from through traffic.[21]

Each coöperative fast freight line had a Board of Directors composed of a representative from each coöperating road. The function of the Board was to decide policy for the line, and the relative weight of each representative's vote was decided either on the basis of the length of his road or on the basis of the proportion of line business which it carried. This board had no jurisdiction over freight rates; such rates continued to be set by the individual railroads or by agreement among all the roads in the line.[22] A general office was maintained by each coöperative line, and was presided over by a general manager. It employed a staff of clerks, and functioned as a clearing house. Headquarters of the Blue Line, for instance, were in Detroit; both the Red and White lines had general offices in Buffalo.[23]

J. D. Hayes, general manager of the Blue Line (which may be regarded as typical of the coöperative lines), testifying before a Senate Committee in 1873, outlined the work of his office. According to Hayes, copies of Blue Line waybills were sent to Detroit where the earnings of the line on each shipment were computed and prorated to the coöperating railroads according to agreement. Hayes's office also had charge of mileage balances. Each coöperating road paid $1\frac{1}{2}$ cents a mile for the use of each Blue Line car not its own that passed over its road. Likewise, any road outside the line that received the line's cars paid mileage of $1\frac{1}{2}$ cents to the line. A record of car movements was kept by the central office and balances were struck once a month.[24] The monthly income of the New York Central from its participation in the Blue Line, therefore, equaled the Central's pro rata share of the earnings of the line less any car mileage the road might owe other roads (or alternatively, plus any mileage other roads might owe the Central, depending upon which total was the larger), less the Central's share of the Line's general office and agents' expenses.

Within a very short time after their first appearance the fast freight lines became remarkably efficient. By 1874 they blanketed the nation and were carrying "substantially all" through freight that moved by rail.[25]

THE PATTERN OF THE FAST FREIGHT LINES

The principal fast freight lines of the 1870's might be grouped according to the trunk lines over which they operated. In 1874 the New York Central participated in four coöperative freight lines: the Red, Blue, White, and International, while the Merchants' Dispatch, a non-coöperative line, also operated over the Central's tracks. A witness appearing before a Congressional committee described the Red Line as running by way of Buffalo over the Lake Shore and Michigan Southern to Chicago, also down the Toledo and Wabash and its branches, "and to various points in what might be called the central part of the Southwest." The Blue Line, according to the same authority, ran over the Great Western and Michigan Central to Chicago and into "what might be called the Northwest." [26] The White Line diverged from the Lake Shore at Cleveland and proceeded through central and southern Ohio, Indiana, and Illinois to St. Louis.[27] The Merchants' Dispatch covered the same territory as the Red, White, and Blue lines. After 1878 the coöperative lines operating over the Central were confined to procuring freight in the west for eastern shipment, while the Merchants' Dispatch took charge of the west bound freight over the Vanderbilt lines.[28]

The Red, Blue, and White lines ran to Boston as well as to New York, leaving the tracks of the Central at Albany and proceeding east by way of the Western and the Boston and Worcester. About 1878 the Hoosac Tunnel Line was organized for the procuring of business for the route through the tunnel. West of Albany this freight line ran over the New York Central and Lake Shore. Also serving Boston was the National Dispatch–Grand Trunk route.[29]

The fast freight lines in which the Erie was chiefly concerned were the Great Western Dispatch and the Erie and North Shore Dispatch. Associated with the Erie in the Great Western Dispatch were the Lake Shore; the Cleveland, Columbus and Cincinnati; the Atlantic and Great Western; the Indianapolis and St. Louis; the Ohio and Mississippi; "and a few lateral lines." [30] The Erie and North Shore Dispatch, the cars of which moved west through Canada, dated from 1872, the year in which the Niagara Falls branch of the Erie Railway was completed. In 1876 three smaller fast freight lines, the Commercial Express, the Diamond, and the Erie and Milwaukee, were absorbed by the Erie and North Shore.[31]

The prinicipal fast freight lines on the Pennsylvania were the Empire, the Star Union, and the National Lines. According to a correspondent of the New York *World*, writing in 1878, each of these lines had its distinct field in the West in which to procure freight for eastern shipment over the Pennsylvania Railroad.[32]

The Continental Fast Freight Line, a coöperative in which the Baltimore and Ohio, the Marietta and Cincinnati, and the Ohio and Mississippi

Railroads were associated was the chief fast freight line operating over the B. and O. By the time of its organization in 1871, the Ohio River had been bridged at Parkersburg and the gauge of the Ohio and Mississippi had been narrowed to conform with that of its eastern connections. Thus, with the inauguration of the Continental Fast Freight Line, "an unbroken communication is opened between Baltimore and St. Louis, giving a new Atlantic port to the . . . West and Southwest." [33]

The principal fast freight line in the area south of trunk line territory was the Green Line, which had been organized in 1868. The original coöperating railroads were the Louisville and Nashville; the Nashville and Northwestern; the Nashville, Chattanooga and St. Louis; and the Western and Atlantic. By 1873 there were twenty-one corporations associated in the Green Line.[34] At this same date there were at least two other fast freight lines in the South, the Crescent (or Mobile and New Orleans) Line and the Great Southern, a line running along the Atlantic seaboard.[35]

The fast freight lines mentioned by name in this section do not constitute a complete roster of such lines, even for the 1870's. An attempt has been made to note only those which were the most important. Nor should the impression that the lines operated only over the roads that have been mentioned as coöperating roads be allowed to stand. The cars of all the freight lines ran by agreement over a great number of roads not actually associated in the lines. In the month of November, 1872, when only twenty railroads were actually coöperating in the Blue Line, the cars of the line ran over 124 different roads.[36] In 1873 it was noted that no southern railroad of importance east of the Mississippi Valley was unaffected by the traffic of the Green Line.[37]

GROWTH AND ABUSES

Largely as a result of the superior functioning of the fast freight lines the amount of grain diverted from water to all-rail routes increased each year. Rail shipment was encouraged, to be sure, by low rates on through freight in contrast to high rates on local traffic to lake ports, but the obvious convenience and relative speed of the fast freights were important factors in their success.[38] Other factors were the institutional reforms for which the fast freight lines were responsible. Most important of these was the regular issuing of through bills of lading, commercial instruments which were largely unknown before 1860.[39] Prior to that time it had been the custom of railroads to issue bills of lading for their own roads only. In the few cases in which through bills were issued they were so hedged about with restrictions that they proved of little practical value.[40] It was this situation, together with the necessity of transshipping, which had made the services of a forwarding firm indispensable to a shipper. The fact that by the end of the 1870's the fast freight lines were guaranteeing the accuracy of their bills of lading is an index to the revolution that they wrought in shipping.

Not only did the fast freight lines take over an ever-increasing share of the grain traffic from the Great Lakes and Erie Canal, but by the mid-1870's, they had also absorbed a considerable amount of traffic once moved by coastwise vessel. The route of the grain trade to Boston, for instance, had been entirely changed. Before the time of the freight lines, grain destined for that city had been shipped by way of the Great Lakes, the Erie Canal, and the Hudson River to New York where it was transshipped to coastwise vessels. In 1874, however, the great bulk of grain was reaching Boston directly from the West in through cars.[41] By 1889 the fast freight lines had at their command some 60,000 cars,[42] most of which were engaged in hauling grain from the West. During the following decade the railroads took away virtually all grain traffic from even the Erie Canal.[43]

By 1877 the earlier non-coöperative fast freight lines had given way completely to either coöperative or company lines. In the latter category belong the Empire, the Union, and the National lines, all the stock of which had been purchased by the Pennsylvania Railroad. By this date also most of the stock of the Merchants' Dispatch was in the hands of the New York Central.[44] Although most early observers agreed that the coöperative fast freight lines were an improvement over the non-coöperative, before long critics discovered evils in the new system. These evils arose principally from competition among the fast freight lines themselves. The large grain traffic of the 1880's led to a multiplication of the number of freight lines, for no railroad or combination of roads could run the risk of losing through freight to a rival road or system. By 1891, Boston, one of the most important grain shipping ports, was being served by thirty-one fast freight lines.[45] In the early days of the lines, when shipping facilities were limited and traffic was to be had simply by providing the necessary cars, the coöperative lines apparently had had no freight agents of their own but had depended upon the agents of their coöperating roads.[46] Later, when they found themselves in competition with other lines, the coöperative lines, like the non-coöperative, hired agents, particularly in the western cities.

In January 1891, it was reported, there were in Chicago alone "more than 20 fast freight line offices, each supporting a force of soliciting agents and clerks." [47] The same authority maintained that in St. Louis, a city with a smaller number of initial roads, fully as many fast freight line offices were maintained as in Chicago. One road with a terminus in St. Louis was not only at the expense of maintaining its own freight agency and solicitors, but also paid its proportion of the expenses of the agencies and solicitors of 10 fast freight lines that operated over its road from that point.[48] These "armies of agents" came to have considerable discretion in the matter of rates, feeling themselves free to undercut the quotations of their competitors. In 1886 one observer questioned whether any other single cause was more responsible for the demoralization of freight rates than the competitive bidding of the freight lines for traffic.[49]

Long before the turn of the century a number of critics, hoping to eradicate the latter-day evils of the freight lines, were urging their abandonment in favor of a nation-wide clearing-house system that would permit the interchange of the cars of all roads.

IX

LAST STEPS IN INTEGRATION, 1880-1890

TOWARD A NATION-WIDE STANDARD GAUGE

During the 1870's, rapid progress toward the adoption of the standard gauge was made all over America except in that part of the South east of the Mississippi River. A few roads, representing a little less than three per cent of total United States mileage, by 1880 had accomplished the change by using a third rail. But a number of railroads of once divergent gauge had made an abrupt change to the standard gauge. This course was taken, for instance, by the 5 foot 6-inch Grand Trunk of Canada in 1874 and by the 6-foot Delaware, Lackawanna and Western in 1876.[1] By 1880 practically all Canadian roads had shifted from the 5 foot 6-inch gauge to standard. In the United States this same broad gauge, which had been common in Missouri and other states south of Missouri and west of the Mississippi River, had also virtually disappeared.[2] Similarly, the 4 foot 10-inch gauge, previously so common in New Jersey and Ohio, had, except for 52 miles, been changed to standard gauge. By 1880 nearly 81 per cent of all the railroad mileage in the United States was equipped to accommodate rolling stock of standard gauge. Of this, 11 per cent of total mileage was of 4 foot 9-inch gauge, which for practical purposes was also standard, since equipment was usually exchanged between roads of these two gauges "without objection."[3] The 5-foot gauge in the South made up 11.4 per cent of the total, leaving 4.8 per cent for the 3-foot lines and about 3 per cent for miscellaneous gauges ranging from 2 to 6 feet.[4]

77

As the data given above indicate, the gauge developments in the South between 1861 and 1880 were quite different on the two sides of the Mississippi River. In the trans-Mississippi Southwest, where most of the earlier roads had been broad gauge, post–Civil War construction was of standard gauge. And the older roads gradually narrowed their trackage in order to facilitate interline exchange with their standard-gauge connections. The Pacific Railroad of Missouri, originally of 5-foot 6-inch gauge, had adopted standard as early as 1869. Of the more than 2900 miles of railroad in the state of Missouri in 1873, only 310 miles were of other than 4-foot 8½-inch gauge. At the same time not a single mile of broad gauge was to be found in Texas.[5]

But east of the Mississippi, where the 5-foot gauge had been most common, the tendency immediately following the war was toward the extension of this gauge. Not only was this width of track used for much new construction, but a few roads which had been built to the standard gauge were now converted to a rail spread of 5 feet. Thus, after a prolonged struggle in which local mercantile interests sought to retain the 4-foot 8½-inch gauge of the North Carolina Railroad, northern investors finally gained control and forced a change to a 5-foot gauge which would facilitate interstate trade.[6] In 1860 the total miles of 5-foot gauge track was 7,267; by 1880 it had increased to 12,137.[7]

Nevertheless, the rapid spread of the standard gauge outside the South and the need to facilitate North-South trade tended gradually to extend the mileage of standard gauge track, especially in southern border states. The first railroad bridge across the Ohio River was completed at Cincinnati in 1870. The inauguration of through traffic across this bridge and the gradual completion of other bridges at Ohio River points increased the pressure on southern railroads to adopt the standard gauge. Chiefly as a result of standard-gauge construction in Virginia, West Virginia, and Kentucky the percentage of total railroad mileage of 5-foot gauge in the South declined slightly between 1860 and 1880.[8] Finally, during the decade of the eighties, the needs of through intersectional trade led to the almost complete abandonment of the divergent southern gauge.

In July 1881, the gauge of the Kentucky Central Railroad was changed from 5 feet to standard because the road formed the link between the standard-gauge Chesapeake and Ohio and the standard-gauge roads which converged on Cincinnati. The *Railroad Gazette,* in accounting for the change gave full credit to the eastward-flowing grain and provision traffic which made uniformity of gauge "almost indispensable." Further, the same source implied that the change of the gauge of the Kentucky Central to standard would force all the railroads in Kentucky to adopt that gauge, for "with a standard-gauge road giving Kentucky its shortest outlet to the sea, it will be desirable that all its roads should be able to interchange cars with it." Nor would the Kentucky roads be unique among the railroads of the South in changing to standard. "Probably all purchases of rolling stock for Southern roads hereafter," prophesied the *Railroad Gazette*, "will be made with regard to a possible future change of gauge." [9]

In 1884 the Illinois Central lines south of the Ohio adopted the standard gauge, bringing the southern end of the Illinois Central into conformity with the northern end and eliminating the necessity of changing the trucks on the cars at Cairo. "Under the pressure of competition," the Mobile and Ohio in July 1885, also changed its line to standard. This left the most direct competitors of the Mobile and Ohio, the Louisville and Nashville and the Cincinnati Southern, with no choice but to make a similar change or be at a disadvantage in bidding for through traffic. Other roads in the South perforce had to act with the Louisville and Nashville and the Cincinnati Southern. [10]

THE SOUTH JOINS THE UNION

On February 2, 1886, representatives of all the important broad-gauge lines in the South met at Atlanta, Georgia, to discuss ways and means of effecting a change of gauge on the more than 13,000 miles of track controlled by their companies. It was decided at this meeting to synchronize the changeover on all the lines. The dates chosen for the project were Monday, May 31, and Tuesday, June 1, 1886. [11]

In line with the prediction of the *Railroad Gazette*, for some time prior to 1886, southern roads had purchased equipment with an eye to its convertibility to a narrower gauge. [12] During the four-month period between the beginning of February and the end of May 1886, part of the rolling stock of the roads was changed to the new gauge so that a supply of cars and motive power would be available when the track gauge was changed. The locomotives of the Southern roads could be more easily converted to standard gauge than could those of the broad gauge roads to the north, for the change in gauge for the Southern roads involved a change of only three inches,[13] as compared with a change of 9½ inches on the Canadian roads and 15½ inches on the Erie. Another factor which kept down the cost of changing the Southern gauge was that the Southern roads, on the whole, had less rolling stock than the Northern roads.[14] Nonetheless, the cost of changing the gauge of the Southern railroads was estimated at $150 a mile, "and on a number of lines more than half of the outlay was for changes in the rolling stock."[15]

In altering the track gauge over such a large area the experience of other roads which had changed gauge in the past was drawn upon. Only one rail, of course, was moved, that rail being shoved inward three inches while the other rail was left undisturbed. Careful preparation was made before the day designated for the changeover. About the beginning of May each road assigned crews to smoothing ties and roadbed and to removing a number of spikes from the rail that was marked for shifting. It should be explained, perhaps, that in the days before tie plates were used the base of the rail was held to each tie by two spikes, one on either side. While the outside spikes were left untouched by the workmen, two-thirds of the inside ones on straight track and every other one on curves were drawn. Then, the distance that the rail was to be set over was measured and new inside spikes driven into every third tie along the new line. All this was accomplished before the end of May.[16]

On the date of the changeover at least three workmen were assigned to each mile of track. On the Louisville and Nashville the quota was at least four men to a mile. Where there were a number of curves or bridges and trestles the quota was raised to five men. As a result of the careful preparations, all that had to be done was to draw the few spikes that remained to hold the rail in its old position, shove the base of the rail under the spikes that had been driven on the inside of the new gauge, and drive in a minimum of spikes to secure the outside of the shifted rail. The remaining work was left to be finished after traffic had been resumed.[17] An example of the speed with which the changeover was accomplished was the record of a Louisville and Nashville section foreman and his gang who changed eleven miles of track in four and a half hours.[18]

Ten roads made the changeover on May 31st: the Louisville and Nashville; the Nashville, Chattanooga and St. Louis; the Memphis and Charleston; the Alabama Great Southern; the Cincinnati Southern; the Cincinnati, Selma and Mobile; the Montgomery and Eufala; the Southwestern and Georgia; the Pensacola and Atlanta; and the Florida Railway and Navigation Company. All other main lines were changed on June 1st. The event was an occasion for a holiday, people traveling many miles in some cases to watch the work crews. On both days the work was completed between 3:30 A.M. and 4 P.M., during which time all train movements were suspended. When traffic was resumed after 4:00 P.M. on June 1, 1886, the American railroad system had become for the first time a physically integrated network.[19] ". . . [A] passenger or freight car could leave Portland, Maine, or Portland, Oregon; San Francisco, Chicago, or any prominent railway centre, and traverse without change of trucks or bulk every mile of southern road leading to New Orleans, Texas, or Florida." [20]

A FOOTNOTE ON GAUGE

Complete uniformity of gauge, however, had not quite been attained by the changeover of the Southern roads to "standard," for the "standard" adopted by those roads in 1886 was 4 feet 9 inches, the gauge of the Pennsylvania Railroad system.[21] The reason for this was that most of the roads had their largest interchange business with the East and Northeast, and consequently with the Pennsylvania and its connections. As was pointed out at that time, "there must necessarily be a large interchange of cars with that road, and it would follow that the gauge used should readily admit Pennsylvania Railroad cars, and that . . . [Southern] cars must be acceptable to that road." [22] For the benefit of the unenlightened, the Charleston *News and Courier* explained that since "a certain amount of lateral play" was allowed on all tracks, a gauge of 4 feet 9 inches was sufficiently near the northern gauge to permit the use of a uniform wheel gauge all over the country.[23] Nonetheless, in the interests of efficiency and safety, the Southern roads in 1886 adopted the "limit gauge" of the Pennsylvania and voted to reject all cars having wheel gauges which measured less than the limits set.[24]

A decade later, in October 1896, the Committee on Standard Wheel and Track Gauges of the American Railway Association recommended that 4 feet 8½ inches be adopted as the track gauge for all American railroads. As late as 1899, however, there were still some 25,000 miles of track of 4 foot 9-inch gauge in the United States. In that year the Master Car

Builders' Association announced that railroad companies representing 82 per cent of the railroad mileage in the United States, Canada, and Mexico had adopted the M. C. B. standard car gauge. This car gauge, while intended as a compromise which would be acceptable to both 4 foot 8½-inch and 4 foot 9-inch roads, as finally "improved and perfected" was admittedly designed for the narrower gauge. The only course left to the 4 foot 9-inch roads was to draw in their track gauge to the 4 foot 8½-inch standard.[25]

The actual lessening of the gauge of the 4 foot 9-inch roads by half an inch took place without fanfare, the adjustment being made whenever track had to be replaced. So gradually was the change accomplished that the precise time at which it was completed is apparently now unknown. In the case of one road, the Louisville and Nashville, "it would seem to have occurred sometime during the year 1900." [26]

THE RAILROAD PATTERN IN 1890

During the thirty years following 1860 railroad mileage in the United States grew more rapidly than during any other period of comparable length in the nation's history. The 30,626 miles of line which the country could claim just prior to the Civil War had expanded by 1890 to almost 160,000 miles.

This striking expansion is immediately apparent to anyone who compares a railroad map of 1890 with one of 1860. Moreover, the map of 1890, unlike that for the earlier date, gives a fair representation of actual conditions, for on maps of 1860 railroads which seemed to be joined were in fact quite separate, but by 1890 technological and institutional improvements had effected a virtual integration of the railroad net. By the beginning of the last decade of the nineteeth century trackage breaks at rivers and in cities had been all but eliminated. Most of the great streams had been repeatedly bridged; where bridges proved unfeasible, as between Detroit and Windsor, efficient car ferries had been introduced. Tracks had been joined in the towns; belt lines had been built through and around the great cities; terminals had been improved; and many lines had been double-tracked to care for increased traffic. By 1890, also, only a negligible percentage of the country's railroads were of other than standard gauge. Rolling stock, both passenger and freight, increasingly equipped with standardized coupling and braking equipment, moved smoothly from line to line. Physical obstacles to the free flow of traffic had been largely eliminated.

Institutional advances had kept pace with technological improvements. Of these only the development of the fast freight lines has been emphasized in the preceding chapters. But there were, of course, many others: the adoption of standard time belts which replaced the confusion caused by use of different local times; the issue of through tickets good over connecting roads and often without the need to change cars, and the practice of using through bills of lading for freight shipments. Again, after the war, most of the small railroad companies steadily became absorbed into great railroad empires. These giant organizations, though subject to recurring financial difficulties and suffering at times from being pawns in the struggle between various promoters and speculators, over the period made substantial strides in perfecting railroad engineering, accounting, and management.

We have seen in the first five chapters of this study how in the age of limited markets before the Civil War the forces of competition had led to the building of railroads designed to serve the exclusive needs of each of the great market cities. The result was an uncoördinated railroad patchwork. The later chapters show how this patchwork was converted into a well-integrated network. Under the leadership of financiers and promoters whose interests transcended local loyalties, there emerged a national economy which, on the one hand, was made possible by the railroads, and which, on the other, moulded the railroads themselves into a unified transportation system.

NOTES

I. FOCUSING THE PROBLEM

1. L. C. A. Knowles, *Economic Development in the Nineteenth Century* (London: George Routledge and Sons, Ltd., 1932), p. 201; *Twelfth Census of the United States, 1900, Manufactures*, part 1, pp. lv and lvii; and Pierre Leroy-Beaulieu, *The United States in the Twentieth Century* (New York: Funk and Wagnalls Company, 1906), pp. 256–257.

2. On technical improvements see: Joseph Nimmo, Jr., *Report on the Internal Commerce of the United States, 1881–82* (Washington: Government Printing Office, 1884), pp. 297–302; and J. L. Ringwalt, *Development of Transportation Systems in the United States* (Philadelphia, 1888), pp. 318–347.

3. *Yearbook of the United States Department of Agriculture, 1899* (Washington: Government Printing Office, 1900), pp. 659–662.

4. This restricted mercantile viewpoint was by no means to be found only in America. Frédéric Bastiat devoted one of his most effective satiric essays to the business interests in Bordeaux who sought to perpetuate a break in the railroad which passed through that city. See "Un Chemin de Fer Negatif," in *Oeuvres Complètes de Frédéric Bastiat* (Paris: Guillaumin et Cie, Libraires, 1854), I, 93–94.

5. *Report of the Joint Special Committee in Relation to the Pennsylvania Railroad*, July 2, 1846, p. 8 (pamphlet in the Lehigh University Library). This pamphlet contains letters from various merchant houses stressing the need for the railroad and also a minority report opposing participation by the city, largely on financial grounds.

6. For an interesting early expression of this viewpoint see *Speech of T. G. Cary on the Use of the Credit of the State for the Hoosac Tunnel*, Massachusetts Senate, May 18, 1853 (pamphlet in the Lehigh University Library).

II. THE RAILROAD MAP, 1861

1. A few important lines were completed during April 1861. For example: The Memphis, Clarksville and Louisville was connected to the Louisville and Nashville at Bowling Green; and the segment of the Mobile and Ohio between Corinth, Mississippi, and Jackson, Tennessee, went into operation.

2. The authors used chiefly the maps in the railroad guides for 1861 and 1862. The titles of the guides changed slightly from year to year.

3. A few good regional maps are available for dates just before or just after the war. See, for example, Frederic L. Paxson, "The Railroads of the 'Old Northwest' before the Civil War," *Transactions of the Wisconsin Academy of Sciences, Arts, and Letters*, vol. XVII, part I (Madison, 1914), p. 266; E. Merton Coulter, *The South During Reconstruction, 1865–1877*, vol. VIII of *A History of the South* (Baton Rouge: Louisiana State University Press, 1947), facing page 236. Special reference

should be made to Robert C. Black, III, *The Railroads of the Confederacy* (Chapel Hill: University of North Carolina Press, 1952). This excellent work, which appeared after the maps for this study had been prepared, contains a very good map of southern railroads showing gauges. The map has proved helpful for purposes of comparison.

4. Even if it were desirable to show these small gauge variations, it would be extremely difficult in many cases because reliable and detailed information is lacking.

5. *Tenth Census of the United States*, 1880, vol. IV: *Transportation*, p. 294.

6. References to gauges in the literature on the subject are not always reliable: thus Caroline E. MacGill in *History of Transportation in the United States before 1860* (Washington: Carnegie Institution of Washington, 1917), p. 550, assigns a 5½-foot gauge to the Ohio and Mississippi instead of a 6-foot gauge.

Perhaps the most common error concerns the gauge of the New York Central. The gauge of this road was 4 feet 8½ inches, not 4 feet 8 inches. Nor was it changed during the Civil War. See, for example, C. R. Fish, "The Northern Railroads, 1861," *American Historical Review*, 22:785 (July 1917); and Thomas Weber, *The Northern Railroads in the Civil War, 1861–1865* (New York: King's Crown Press, 1952), p. 7. The confusion is apparently the result of a misprint on p. 70 in some but not all copies of *Burgess' Railway Directory* for 1861 and an error on p. 64 in *Ashcraft's Railway Directory* for 1862.

7. This was especially true in the cases of some of the short railroads in Louisiana and Texas. The gauge of the Southern (Mississippi) Railroad was apparently changed from 4 feet 10 inches to 5 feet, either just before or during the war. The evidence is conflicting. See, for example, *The Engineer*, 1:97 (Nov. 8, 1860); *Burgess' Railway Directory* for 1861, p. 180; and *Ashcraft's Railway Directory* for 1862, p. 140.

8. The directories used chiefly were *Ashcraft's Railway Directory, Burgess' Railway Directory, Low's Railway Directory*, and *Low and Burgess' Railway Directory*. Useful for checking and comparison were *King's Railway Directory for 1867* (New York: A. H. King, 1867); James H. Lyles, *Official Railway Manual of the Railroads of North America for 1869–70* (New York: Thitchener and Glastaeter, 1870), and Henry Varnum Poor, *History of the Railroads and Canals of the United States . . .* (New York: John H. Schultz and Co., 1860).

9. Henry Grote Lewin, *Early British Railways* (New York: Spon and Chamberlain, 1925), pp. 5, 8, 12, 26, and 89. Undoubtedly greater extremes existed in both directions. In 1846 the gauge of British tramways was reported to vary from 2 feet to 4 feet 8½ inches. *Journal of the Franklin Institute of the State of Pennsylvania*, Third Series, 12:298 (November 1846), quoting the *Mining Journal*.

10. *American State Papers, Miscellaneous*, I (Washington: Gales and Seaton, 1834), 916.

11. See, for example, *Journal of the Franklin Institute of the State of Pennsylvania*, Third Series, 13:15–16 (January 1847), quoting *The London Railway Magazine; Yearbook of the United States Department of Agriculture, 1899* (Washington: Government Printing Office, 1900), p. 652; Robert R. Brown, "Gauges — Standard and Otherwise," *The Railway and Locomotive Historical Society*, Bulletin No. 88 (May 1953), p. 81; MacGill, *History of Transportation in the United States before 1860*, p. 313; Richard B. Osborne, *Is There any Reason Why the Present Gauge of our Iron Roads should be Adopted on our Future Railways?* (Baltimore: Kelly, Piet

and Co., 1871), p. 3 (pamphlet in Baker Library of Harvard University); and Horatio Allen, *The Railroad Era, First Five Years of its Development* (New York: 1884), pp. 30–31 (pamphlet).

12. Considerable attention was paid in the United States to this controversy. See, for example, *Journal of the Franklin Institute of the State of Pennsylvania*, Third Series, 12:225–234 (October 1846), and continued in subsequent numbers.

13. *Journal of the Franklin Institute of the State of Pennsylvania*, Third Series, 12:298 (November 1846), and *American Railway Review*, 2:326 (May 31, 1860).

14. *The American Railway Times*, 13:186 (May 11, 1861).

15. *American Rail-Road Journal*, 1:51 (January 21, 1832); and *The Rail-Road Advocate*, 1:138–139 (February 28, 1832), and 1:145 (March 15, 1832).

16. *American Railway Review*, 2:326 (May 31, 1860).

III. NEW ENGLAND AND CANADA, 1861

1. Boston Board of Trade, *Third Annual Report* (Boston, 1857), p. 28; and Edward Chase Kirkland, *Men, Cities and Transportation* (Cambridge, Mass., Harvard University Press, 1948), I, 139–147.

2. *American Railway Review*, 2:4 (December 1, 1859).

3. Kirkland, *Men, Cities and Transportation*, I, 137–138; and Boston Board of Trade, *Second Annual Report* (Boston, 1856), p. 17. During the summer westward shipments from Boston were also made by a circuitous route through Rutland, Vermont, and then to Schenectady where they continued via the Eria Canal. *Ibid.*, p. 20.

4. *Ibid.*, pp. 20–21; Kirkland, *Men, Cities and Transportation*, I, 158–191; and G. P. de T. Glazebrook, *A History of Transportation in Canada* (Toronto: The Ryerson Press, 1938), p. 165.

5. The story of railroad development in Maine is well told in Kirkland, *Men, Cities and Transportation*, I, chapter vii.

6. *American Railway Review*, 1:10 (November 17, 1859), quoted from *Boston Transcript*, November 8, 1859.

7. Edmund F. Webb, ed. *The Railroad Laws of Maine* (Portland, Maine: Dresser, McLellan and Co., 1875), p. 14.

8. A. C. Morton, *Report on the Gauge for the St. Lawrence and Atlantic Railroad* (Portland: Thurston and Co., 1847).

9. Laura Elizabeth Poor, ed., *The First International Railway and the Colonization of New England: Life and Writings of John Alfred Poor* (New York: G. P. Putnam's Sons, 1892), pp. 50–51.

10. Webb, ed., *The Railroad Laws of Maine*, p. 629. See also John A. Poor, *No Restrictions on Railway Transit. Argument of John A. Poor before the Joint Standing Committee on Railroads, Ways and Bridges* (Bangor, Maine: David Bugbee and Co., 1865), pp. 6–7, 24–25; and Boston Board of Trade, *Eleventh Annual Report* (Boston, 1865), pp. 40–42.

11. Kirkland, *Men, Cities and Transportation*, I, 215–218.

12. Frank Walker Stevens, *The Beginnings of the New York Central Railroad* (New York: G. P. Putnam's Sons, 1926), pp. 342–346; Thomas C. Keefer, "Travel and Transportation" in *Eighty Years' Progress of British North America* (Toronto:

L. Stebbins, 1863), pp. 253–254; Henry B. Gibson to Erastus Corning, Canandaigua, New York, March 24, 1852, and same to same, June 14, 1852, in Corning Papers, Albany Institute of History and Art, Albany, New York.

13. Keefer, "Travel and Transportation" in *Eighty Years' Progress of British North America*, pp. 245–246.

14. *Ibid.*, pp. 194 and 253.

15. On the early railroads of Canada and the Maritime Provinces see Glazebrook, *A History of Transportation in Canada*, chapter v; and Norman Thompson and Major J. H. Edgar, *Canadian Railway Development from the Earliest Times* (Toronto: The Macmillan Company of Canada, 1933).

16. *Low and Burgess' Railway Directory*, 1860, p. 176.

17. *American Railway Review*, 1:6 (November 17, 1859), and 2:6 (December 1, 1859).

IV. THE MIDDLE ATLANTIC STATES, 1861

1. But not including the Ogdensburg Railroad (also called The Northern), for this line, as already indicated, formed part of the rival New England system. New York merchants had gone to considerable lengths to prevent the building of a bridge to carry this railroad across the northern end of Lake Champlain. See J. B. Varnum, "Railroad Legislation of New York in 1849," *Hunt's Merchants' Magazine*, 21:171–177 (August 1849).

2. Frank Walker Stevens, *The Beginnings of the New York Central Railroad, A History* (New York: G. P. Putnam's Sons, 1926); Harry H. Pierce, *Railroads of New York, A Study of Government Aid, 1836–1875* (Cambridge: Harvard University Press, 1953), especially chapters 1 and 4; and David Maldwyn Ellis, "Albany and Troy — Commercial Rivals," *New York History*, 24:484–511 (October 1943).

3. Some of the roads which united to form the New York Central were not originally built to a gauge of 4 feet 8½ inches. Thus, the Mohawk and Hudson had been constructed with its rails 4 feet 9 inches apart. Stevens, *The Beginnings of the New York Central Railroad*, p. 33.

4. But the legislature soon granted exceptions to this restriction.

5. Edward Harold Mott, *Between the Ocean and the Lakes, The Story of Erie* (New York: John S. Collins, 1901), pp. 44–45. When in the middle 1840's plans were being made for building the Western Division of the Erie, the consulting engineer for the road recommended a five-foot gauge, but the board of directors voted against any change. *Ibid.*, p. 45; and Horatio Allen, *The Railroad Era, First Five Years of its Development* (New York: 1884), p. 31 (pamphlet).

6. Jules I. Bogen, *The Anthracite Railroads* (New York: The Ronald Press, 1927), pp. 83–84; Wheaton J. Lane, *From Indian Trail to Iron Horse, Travel and Transportation in New Jersey 1620–1860* (Princeton: Princeton University Press, 1939), p. 387.

7. On New Jersey railroads, see especially Lane, *From Indian Trail to Iron Horse, Travel and Transportation in New Jersey 1620–1860*. The Camden and Atlantic Railroad, another standard-gauge railroad, connected Philadelphia and Atlantic City. It belonged to the Philadelphia system, however, rather than to that of New York.

8. L. 1852, No. 36. Cf. Frederick A. Cleveland and Fred Wilbur Powell, *Railroad Promotion and Capitalization in the United States* (New York: Longman's,

Green, and Co., 1909), p. 126; Edward Hungerford, *Men of Erie* (New York: Random House, 1946), pp. 34–37; and Robert J. Casey and W. A. S. Douglas, *The Lackawanna Story* (New York: McGraw-Hill Book Co., 1951), chapters 8 and 10.

9. On the coal roads, see Bogen, *The Anthracite Railroad*, and *A Century of Progress, History of the Delaware and Hudson Company 1823–1923* (Albany: J. B. Lyon Company, 1925).

10. The southern counties came to the support of Baltimore.

11. James Weston Livingood, *The Philadelphia-Baltimore Trade Rivalry 1780–1860* (Harrisburg: The Pennsylvania Historical and Museum Commission, 1947), chapters vi and vii; and George H. Burgess and Miles C. Kennedy, *Centennial History of the Pennsylvania Railroad Company* (Philadelphia: The Pennsylvania Railroad Company, 1949), pp. 128–138.

12. *Ibid.*, p. 37.

13. But by no means did all the funds come from private sources. It was reported in the *Annual Report of the Pennsylvania Railroad Company*, Feb. 2, 1857, p. 6, that nearly one-half of the company's stock was owned by the city of Philadelphia and Allegheny County.

14. See *Annual Report of the Pennsylvania Railroad Company*, Feb. 2, 1857, pp. 35–39; and Edward Hungerford, *The Story of the Baltimore and Ohio Railroad, 1827–1927* (New York: G. P. Putnam's Sons, 1928), I, 249–250; *Niles' National Register*, 69:96 (October 11, 1845).

15. *History of the Railway Mail Service*, 48th Congress, 2nd Session, Senate Exec. Document No. 40, p. 59; and *Annual Report of the Pennsylvania Railroad Company*, February 7, 1859, pp. 3–5 and 15–16.

16. *Improved Railway Connections in Philadelphia* (Philadelphia: James H. Bryson, 1863), p. 3 (pamphlet in the Boston Public Library).

17. *The Merchants' Magazine*, 46:39 (January 1862). See also *Improved Railway Connections in Philadelphia; The Merchants' Magazine*, 46:73–74 (January 1862); William Ferguson, *America by River and Rail* (London: James Nisbet and Company, 1856), pp. 94, 223; Joseph P. Bradley, William Wheeler Hubbell, and George Ashmun, *Considerations upon the Question Whether Congress Should Authorize a New Railroad between Washington and New York* (New York: G. S. Gideon and Company, 1863); *Congressional Globe*, February 7, 1863, p. 773, and February 11, 1863, p. 886; and *Statement Made by the Railroad Companies Owning the Lines between Washington and New York to the Postmaster General* (Washington: Gideon and Pearson, 1863).

18. *American Railroad Journal*, 17:6 (January 5, 1861), and 17:301 (April 13, 1861); Ferguson, *America by River and Rail*, p. 98.

19. John W. Brooks, *The Pro Rata Question, What is the True Policy of the State of New York?* (Albany: Weed, Parsons and Company, 1869), p. 15.

20. John W. Garrett, President, Baltimore and Ohio Railroad Co., to Edwin M. Stanton, Secretary of War, February 9, 1862, 37th Congress, 2nd Session, House Exec. Document No. 79, p. 4.

21. See especially Hungerford, *The Story of the Baltimore and Ohio Railroad*, vol. I; Livingood, *The Philadelphia-Baltimore Trade Rivalry*, chapters vii and viii; Burgess and Kennedy, *Centennial History of the Pennsylvania Railroad Company*, pp. 128–138; and Boston Board of Trade, *Second Annual Report* (Boston 1856), pp. 14–15.

22. L. 1851, No. 122.

23. This repeal was stoutly denounced by Philadelphia merchants. See Philadelphia Board of Trade, *Twenty-First Annual Report*, February 6, 1854, pp. 5–6.

24. This story has been told often. One of the best accounts is to be found in Donald H. Kent, "The Erie War of the Gauges," *Pennsylvania History*, 15:253–275 (October 1948).

25. Philadelphia Board of Trade, *Twenty-First Annual Report*, February 6, 1854, pp. 35–36; see also, pp. 5, 6, 20–23, and 34–36.

26. After some delay caused by local interests. See *Tenth Annual Report of the Pennsylvania Railroad Company*, February 2, 1857, p. 13.

27. See pp. 59–60.

28. Rolland Harper Maybee, *Railroad Competition and the Oil Trade 1855–1873* (New York: Extension Press, Central State Teachers' College, 1940), p. 81.

29. Hungerford, *The Story of the Baltimore and Ohio Railroad*, I, 265–266, 293; Boston Board of Trade, *Second Annual Report* (Boston, 1856), pp. 14–16, and *Third Annual Report* (Boston, 1857), p. 22.

30. Hungerford, *The Story of the Baltimore and Ohio Railroad*, I, 293–296; Joseph Nimmo, Jr., *Report on the Internal Commerce of the United States* (Washington: Government Printing Office, 1881), Appendix, pp. 234–235.

31. *The Merchants' Magazine*, 44:370 (March 1861).

V. MIDWEST AND SOUTH, 1861

1. See, for example, Charles Frederick Carter, *When Railroads Were New* (New York: Simons-Boardman Publishing Co., 1926), pp. 220–222; Robert L. Black, *The Little Miami Railroad* (Cincinnati, Ohio: n.d.), p. 32; and J. E. Glover, *The Click of the Rails* (Jackson, Tenn.: The Railroader, Publishers, 1929), p. 15.

2. *Annual Report of the* (Ohio) *Commission of Railroads and Telegraphs for the year 1870* (Columbus, Ohio: Nevins and Myers, 1870), I, 21.

3. *Ibid.*, p. 27.

4. *Ibid.*, pp. 532 and 561.

5. *The Engineer*, 1:61 (October 4, 1860); and *The Railroad Record*, 8:510–511 (December 13, 1860).

6. The General Railroad Law of the state of Missouri, adopted February 24, 1853, required all roads to be built to a gauge of 5 feet 6 inches but, like the similar legislation which established an official gauge for Ohio, seems to have had little effect. *An Act to Authorize the Formation of Railroad Associations* (St. Louis: The Missouri Democrat, 1854), p. 14.

7. Charles Henry Ambler, *A History of Transportation in the Ohio Valley* (Glendale, California: The Arthur H. Clark Co., 1932), pp. 211–212; and Louis C. Hunter, *Steamboats on the Western Rivers* (Cambridge: Harvard University Press, 1949), pp. 594–595.

8. Ambler, *A History of Transportation in the Ohio Valley*, pp. 212–230.

9. Wylie J. Daniels, *The Village at the End of the Road, A Chapter in Early Indiana Railroad History* (Indianapolis: Indiana Historical Society, 1938), pp. 99–100.

10. Walter Smith, *Annual Review of the Commerce of Cincinnati* (Cincinnati: 1864), p. 12.

11. Boston Board of Trade, *Third Annual Report* (Boston, 1857), pp. 23–24; George H. Burgess and Miles C. Kennedy, *Centennial History of the Pennsylvania Railroad Company* (Philadelphia: The Pennsylvania Railroad Company, 1949), pp. 176–179. Through shipment from Buffalo to Chicago without change of gauge was also possible via the so-called Cleveland, Crestline and Chicago Route. The gauge of this route, which used the tracks of the Cleveland, Crestline and Chicago Railroad from Cleveland to Crestline, and that of the Pittsburgh, Fort Wayne and Chicago from Crestline to Chicago, was 4 feet 10 inches throughout. *American Railway Review*, 2:7 (December 1, 1859).

12. Boston Board of Trade, *Second Annual Report* (Boston, 1856), pp. 14–15; Edward Hungerford, *The Story of the Baltimore and Ohio Railroad* (New York: G. P. Putnam's Sons, 1928), I, 325–326.

13. *American Railway Review*, 3:251 (October 25, 1860).

14. Hungerford, *The Story of the Baltimore and Ohio*, I, 298–301.

15. Though Missouri railroads were of two gauges, no evidence has come to light which would indicate that this situation was deliberately created or continued because of commercial rivalry.

16. Frank Haigh Dixon, *A Traffic History of the Mississippi River System* (Washington: Government Printing Office, 1917), p. 32.

17. Arthur Charles Cole, *The Era of the Civil War, 1848–1870*, vol. III of *The Centennial History of Illinois* (Springfield, Illinois: Illinois Centennial Commission, 1919), pp. 32–36, 43–46; Wyatt Winton Belcher, *The Economic Rivalry between St. Louis and Chicago 1850–1880* (New York: Columbia University Press, 1947), pp. 92–95.

18. Whether St. Louisians favored the 6-foot gauge adopted for this road, and if so, whether for motives of excluding competition, is not known.

19. W. B. Baker, *Annual Statement of the Trade and Commerce of St. Louis for the Year 1858* (St. Louis, Missouri: Baker and Hildreth, 1859), pp. 5–6. See also *American Railway Review*, 3:245 (October 25, 1860); and William F. Switzler, *Report on the Internal Commerce of the United States*, part II of *Commerce and Navigation, Special Report on the Commerce of the Mississippi, Ohio, and Other Rivers, and of the Bridges Which Cross Them*, Treasury Department Document No. 1039b, Bureau of Statistics (Washington: Government Printing Office, 1888), pp. 19–25.

20. *American Railway Review*, 3:87 (August 16, 1860), and 3:393 (December 27, 1860).

21. Bessie Louise Pierce, *A History of Chicago* (New York: Alfred A. Knopf, 1940), II, 41–43; Belcher, *The Economic Rivalry Between St. Louis and Chicago 1850–1880*, pp. 62–64.

22. *Charleston Courier*, March 13, 1828, as quoted in Samuel Melanchthon Derrick, *Centennial History of South Carolina Railroad* (Columbia, S.C.: The State Co., 1930), p. 19. On the role of local interests in the early construction of Southern railroads see Milton S. Heath, "North American Railroads: Public Railroad Construction and the Development of Private Enterprise in the South Before 1861," *Journal of Economic History*, Supplement X (1950), 43–45.

23. The point probably should be made, as suggested by Robert M. Sutton, that the federal land grant of 1850 to Illinois, Mississippi, and Alabama was the only action taken by the government before the Civil War which even remotely suggested a national transportation policy. Here was an attempt to provide rail transportation

between the Lakes and the Gulf. But the policy was not fully realized because there was a difference in gauge between the Illinois Central and the southern roads and because it was necessary to resort to the river between Columbus and Cairo.

24. A small gap between Corinth and Jackson remained on the Mobile and Ohio until April 22, 1861. On New Orleans–Mobile rivalry see R. S. Cotterill, "Southern Railroads, 1850–1860," *Mississippi Valley Historical Review*, 10:396–401 (March 1924).

25. *American Railroad Journal*, 17:264 (March 30, 1861); and U. B. Phillips, *A History of Transportation in the Eastern Cotton Belt to 1860* (New York: Columbia University Press, 1908), pp. 359–361.

26. Cecil Kenneth Brown, *A State Movement in Railroad Development* (Chapel Hill: The University of North Carolina Press, 1928), pp. 66–69, 164–165; Samuel A. Ashe *et al.*, eds., *Biographical History of North Carolina* (Greensboro, N.C.: Charles L. Van Noppen, 1917), VIII, 33.

27. Horatio Allen, *The Railroad Era, First Five Years of its Development* (New York, 1884), p. 31 (pamphlet); Derrick, *Centennial History of South Carolina Railroad*, p. 40.

28. This was changed to 5 feet just before or during the war. The exact date has proved impossible to determine.

29. Brown, *A State Movement in Railroad Development*, p. 18.

30. *Ibid.*, pp. 18–19, 22–23, 36, 137, 166–168, 179–181; and "A History of the Piedmont Railroad Company," *North Carolina Historical Review*, 3:198–222 (April 1926).

31. Robert C. Black, III, *The Railroads of the Confederacy* (Chapel Hill: University of North Carolina Press, 1952), pp. 9, 73–74.

32. See *Colton's Atlas of the World* (New York: J. H. Colton and Co., 1855), vol. 1, plate 28; and *Atlas to Accompany the Official Records of the Union and Confederate Armies* (Washington, Government Printing Office, 1891–1895), plate 70.

33. Letter from Major W. S. Ashe to Jefferson Davis, November 27, 1861. C. S. Railroad Documents, War Department Collection of Confederate Records, War Records Division, National Archives, cited in Robert C. Black, *The Railroads of the Confederacy*, p. 9. See also Derrick, *Centennial History of South Carolina Railroad*, pp. 118–119; Phillips, *A History of Transportation in the Eastern Cotton Belt to 1860*, pp. 162–163, 207–208, 216; and *Savannah Republican*, November 11, 1861, cited in C. W. Ramsdell, "Confederate Government and the Railroads," *American Historical Review*, 22:797 (July 1917).

34. See *Atlas to Accompany the Official Records of the Union and Confederate Armies*, plates 23, 25 and 132; and *Colton's Atlas of the World*, vol. 1, plate 28.

35. *The War of the Rebellion, A Compilation of the Official Records of the Union and Confederate Armies*, series IV, vol. I, p. 486; see also pp. 394, 405–406, 417–418, 484–486.

36. The references in the preceding footnote also deal with the Richmond problem. On the position of Norfolk in these inter-city rivalries see Thomas J. Wertenbaker, *Norfolk: Historic Southern Port* (Durham: Duke University Press, 1931), pp. 192–203.

VI. THE TREND TOWARD INTEGRATION, 1861–1870

1. For a first-hand account of shipping methods in this period, see the testimony of E. D. Worcester in 43rd Congress, 1st Session (1873–74), Senate Report No. 307, Part 2, p. 130.

2. A. C. Morton, *Report on the Gauge for the St. Lawrence and Atlanta Railroad* (Portland: Thurston and Company, 1847), pp. 20–21.

3. George Dartnell, *A Proposed Plan for a Rail Road Clearing House* (Buffalo: Clapp, Matthews and Co's Steam Printing House, 1858), pp. 11–12.

4. *Congressional Globe*, 37th Congress, 3rd Session, Part 2, p. 1048.

5. *Ibid.*, p. 1046.

6. Patrick Barry, *Over the Atlantic and Great Western Railway* (London: S. Low, son, & Marston, 1866), pp. 62–64, 66–67.

7. *The Resources and Prospects of America Ascertained during a Visit to the States in the Autumn of 1865* (London and New York, 1866), p. 277.

8. See pp. 31–32.

9. *Congressional Globe*, 37th Congress, 3rd Session, Part 2, p. 1047.

10. *Commercial and Financial Chronicle*, 13:210 (August 12, 1871).

11. Boston Board of Trade, *Third Annual Report* (Boston, 1857), p. 27; *Twelfth Annual Report* (1866), p. 70; *Congressional Globe*, 37th Congress, 3rd Session, Part 2, p. 1048. Seven cents a ton for the cost of transshipment may well have been on the low side. George Dartnell stated in 1858 that the cost of transshipment was twenty-five cents a ton and the delay amounted to about twenty-four hours. *A Proposed Plan for a Rail Road Clearing House*, p. 11.

12. Robert C. Black, III, *The Railroads of the Confederacy* (Chapel Hill: University of North Carolina Press, 1952), and Thomas Weber, *The Northern Railroads in the Civil War, 1861–1865* (New York: King's Crown Press, Columbia University, 1952), cover this period in detail.

13. Black, *The Railroads of the Confederacy*, pp. 72–77, 148–163, discusses the building of these and other links in the South during the war years.

14. *New York Times*, February 6, 1863.

15. *Ibid.*, January 21, 1863.

16. *Ibid.*, January 21, and February 5 and 6, 1863; and *Improved Railway Connections in Philadelphia* (Philadelphia: James H. Bryson, 1863), pamphlet in Boston Public Library.

17. *Twenty-Sixth Annual Report of the President and Directors to the Stockholders of the Philadelphia, Wilmington and Baltimore Railroad Company* (Philadelphia: James H. Bryson and Son, 1864), p. 14. See also J. L. Ringwalt, *Development of Transportation Systems in the United States* (Philadelphia: Railway World Office, 1888), pp. 188–189.

18. On the use of steam engines on city streets in Boston and New York see *American Railway Times*, 16:166 (May 21, 1864), and *American Railroad Journal*, 18:537 (July 12, 1862).

19. Boston Board of Trade, *Eleventh Annual Report* (Boston, 1865), pp. 40–41; Weber, *The Northern Railroads in the Civil War, 1861–1865*, pp. 15–17. Chapter II of Weber's volume is concerned with railroad construction in the North during the war.

20. Boston Board of Trade, *Eleventh Annual Report* (Boston, 1865), p. 41.

21. *Ibid.*

22. *Congressional Globe*, 37th Congress, 3rd Session, Part 2, pp. 958–960, and 1046–1049.

23. *Ibid.*, p. 959. See also Silas Seymour, *A Review of the Theory of Narrow Gauges* (New York: D. Van Nostrand, 1871), pp. 23–24.

24. *Congressional Globe*, 37th Congress, 3rd Session, Part 1, p. 492.

25. *Congressional Globe*, 37th Congress, 3rd Session, Part 2, p. 1049.

26. *Ibid.*, p. 1484.

27. George Rogers Taylor, *The Transportation Revolution, 1815–1860*, The Economic History of the United States, IV (New York: Rinehart and Company, 1951), p. 167.

28. Freight rates on wheat from Chicago to New York in 1870 were 26.11 cents a bushel by rail and 19.58 cents by rail and water. *Yearbook of the United States Department of Agriculture, 1899* (Washington: Government Printing Office, 1900), p. 660.

29. Taylor, *The Transportation Revolution, 1815–1860*, p. 167.

30. *American Railway Review*, 3:155 (September, 1860).

31. Philadelphia Board of Trade, *Twenty-eighth Annual Report* (Philadelphia, 1861), pp. 63–64.

32. Philadelphia Board of Trade, *Thirty-second Annual Report* (Philadelphia, 1865), p. 39.

33. See Louis Bernard Schmidt, "The Internal Grain Trade of the United States," *Iowa Journal of History and Politics*, 19:196–245 (April 1921), 19:414–455 (July 1921), and 20:70–131 (January 1922).

VII. SOLVING THE GAUGE DIFFERENTIALS, 1860–1880

1. In 1876 the Empire and the Green Fast Freight Lines, both controlled by the Pennsylvania Railroad, owned over 4500 cars of compromise gauge. *Theory and Practice of the American System of Through Fast Freight Transportation as Illustrated in the Operation of the Empire Transportation Company* (Philadelphia: Helfenstein, Lewis and Greene, 1876), p. 16.

2. Silas Seymour, *A Review of the Theory of Narrow Gauges* (New York: D. Van Nostrand, 1871), p. 23.

3. Charles S. Tisdale to Lorenzo Sabine, Boston, November 2, 1863, as quoted in Boston Board of Trade, *Tenth Annual Report* (Boston, 1864), pp. 33–34; Boston Board of Trade, *Eleventh Annual Report* (Boston 1865), p. 40.

4. *American Railroad Journal*, 29:1329 (October 18, 1873), and 30:1572–1573 (December 5, 1874); Edward C. Kirkland, *Men, Cities and Transportation* (Cambridge: Harvard University Press, 1948), I, 445.

5. 43rd Congress, 1st Session (1873–74), Senate Report No. 307, Part 2, p. 117.

6. Carlton J. Corliss, *Main Line of Mid-America; the Story of the Illinois Central* (New York: Creative Age Press, 1950), pp. 205–206; *Railroad Gazette*, Fifth Quarto Volume (April 12, 1873), p. 146.

7. *Ibid.*

8. *American Railroad Journal*, 30:1573 (December 5, 1874); Edward Harold Mott, *Between the Ocean and the Lakes, the Story of Erie* (New York: John S. Collins, 1901), pp. 227, 234.

9. E. Lavoinne et E. Pontzen, *Les Chemins de Fer en Amerique* (Paris: Libraire des Corps des Ponts et Chaussées et des Mines, 1882), I, 425–426.

10. Kincaid A. Herr, *The Louisville & Nashville Railroad, 1850–1942* (Louisville: L & N Magazine, 1943), p. 46.

11. *Ibid.*

12. *Ibid.*, pp. 46, 76; and *Railroad Gazette*, Nineteenth Quarto Volume (October 14, 1887), p. 668.

13. *Congressional Globe*, 37th Congress, 3rd Session, Part 2, p. 959.

14. *American Railroad Journal*, 29:928 (June 21, 1873).

15. *Ibid.*, 30:1541 (December 5, 1874).

16. *Ibid.*, 30:1573 (December 5, 1874).

17. *Ibid.*, 29:928 (June 21, 1873); Mott, *Between the Ocean and the Lakes*, pp. 147–148.

18. *American Railroad Journal*, 33:36 (January 13, 1877); *ibid.*, 36:25 (January 2, 1880).

19. *Ibid.*, 29:928 (June 21, 1873); Alfred F. Sears, *On Small Gauge Railroads: A Paper read before the Board of Directors of the Pennsylvania and Sodus Bay Railroad Company* (Seneca Falls, 1871), pp. 7–8.

20. Blue Line, *General Manager's Report for the Year 1867* (Detroit, 1868), p. 10.

21. Boston Board of Trade, *Eleventh Annual Report* (Boston, 1865), p. 41.

22. *American Railroad Journal*, 29:1329 (October 18, 1873).

23. For a description of the method used by the Louisville and Nashville Railroad to narrow the gauge of their locomotives in 1886 see Herr, *Louisville & Nashville Railroad*, pp. 47, 48.

24. *Tenth Census of the United States*, 1880, vol. IV, *Transportation*, p. 294. When a double gauge had been formed by means of a third rail, the compilers of the census reduced the third rail to equivalent track (that is, divided the length of the rail by two) and *added* that figure to the trackage of the railroad. Therefore, double-gauge *mileage* was considerably less than it would appear to have been from a hasty first reading of the census figures. Adjustments have been made in the statistics given above.

25. *Railroad Gazette*, Fifteenth Quarto Volume (October 12, 1883), p. 674.

26. The literature of this subject is voluminous. See especially *Commercial and Financial Chronicle*, 15:52 (July 13, 1872); and *American Railroad Journal*, 28:939 (July 27, 1872).

27. Quoted in *American Railroad Journal*, 27:598 (June 3, 1871).

28. *Ibid.*, 28:875 (July 13, 1872).

29. *New York Times*, as quoted in *American Railroad Journal*, 27:629 (June 10, 1871).

30. *American Railroad Journal*, 30:1467 (November 14, 1874).

31. *Ibid.*, 34:492 (May 4, 1878).

32. *Tenth Census of the United States*, 1880, vol. IV, *Transportation*, p. 294.

33. *Railroad Gazette*, Fifteenth Quarto Volume (October 12, 1883), p. 674.

34. *Ibid.*, p. 674.

35. *Ibid.*, Sixteenth Quarto Volume (April 11, 1884), p. 281.

36. *American Railroad Journal*, 30:1573 (December 5, 1874).

VIII. THE FAST FREIGHT LINES, 1861–1890

1. *Commercial and Financial Chronicle*, 8:584 (May 8, 1869).

2. Michigan Central Railroad Company, *Annual Report* (Detroit, 1869), p. 6. (Italics added.)

3. *Ibid.*, 1873, p. 21.

4. *Ibid.*, 1869, p. 6.

5. Buffalo Board of Trade, *Annual Statement* (Buffalo, 1855), p. 38.

6. The 1000 cars with sliding wheels which were operating over the Grand Trunk and its connections in the early 1870's were the property of the National Dispatch, a fast freight line. Edward C. Kirkland, *Men, Cities and Transportation* (Cambridge: Harvard University Press, 1948), I, 445.

7. Blue Line, *General Manager's Report for the Year 1867* (Detroit, 1868), p. 10. The cars were transported across the river between Winsor and Detroit by means of a steam ferry.

8. J. L. Ringwalt, *Development of Transportation Systems in the United States* (Philadelphia: Railway World Office, 1888), p. 193.

9. L. D. H. Weld, "Private Freight Cars and American Railways," Columbia University, *Studies in Political Science*, vol. XXXI, No. 1 (1908), p. 76.

10. Boston Board of Trade, *Second Annual Report* (Boston, 1856), p. 19; *Railway World*, 4:745 (August 3, 1878).

11. *Railway Review*, 30:22 (January 11, 1890); Weld, "Private Freight Cars and American Railways," p. 76; Grover G. Huebner and Emory R. Johnson, *The Railroad Freight Service* (New York: D. Appleton and Company, 1926), p. 94. For a detailed account of the Star Union Line see Huebner and Johnson, pp. 94–96.

12. Huebner and Johnson, *The Railroad Freight Service*, p. 97; Kirkland, *Men, Cities and Transportation*, I, 441–442.

13. 43rd Congress, 1st Session (1873–74), Senate Report No. 307, Part 1, p. 77.

14. Hudson E. Bridge, *The Pacific Railroad Controversy, an Open Letter to the Stockholders: With a Series of Articles Originally Published in the Daily Missouri Democrat* (St. Louis: Missouri Democrat Printing House, 1869), pp. 15–21 (second pagination); Testimony of G. R. Blanchard, 2nd vice-president, Erie Railway Company, 43rd Congress, 1st Session (1873–74), Senate Report No. 307, Part 2, pp. 361–362; Huebner and Johnson, *The Railroad Freight Service*, pp. 96–97.

15. Bridge, *The Pacific Railroad Controversy*, pp. 15–21 (second pagination).

16. Testimony of Joseph D. Potts, president, Empire Fast-Freight Line, 43rd Congress, 1st Session (1873–74), Senate Report No. 307, Part 2, p. 26; Huebner and Johnson, *The Railroad Freight Service*, pp. 96–97.

17. Testimony of G. R. Blanchard, 2nd vice-president, Erie Railway Company, 43rd Congress, 1st Session (1873–74), Senate Report No. 307, Part 2, p. 362.

18. Boston Board of Trade, *Twelfth Annual Report* (Boston, 1866), p. 69; *American Railroad Journal*, 23:703 (July 27, 1867). The cooperative lines were often, though not always, designated by a color, such as the Red Line, the Blue Line, or the Green Line. The White Line, which ran west of St. Louis over the Pacific Railroad, was organized and operated for some time as a non-cooperative line. Bridge, *The Pacific Railroad Controversy*, pp. 14–15 (second pagination).

19. William H. Joubert, *Southern Freight Rates in Transition* (Gainesville: University of Florida Press, 1949), p. 32.

20. Charles A. Sindall, "The Development of the Traffice between the Southern States and the Northern and Northwestern States," 49th Congress, 2nd Session (1886–87), House Executive Document No. 7, Part 2, p. 681.

21. *Railroad Gazette*, Third Quarto Volume (November 29, 1873), p. 478; 43rd Congress, 1st Session (1873–74), Senate Report No. 307, Part 1, p. 77.

22. An exception to this occurred in the South where freight rates on some through traffic carried by the Green Line were set by a committee composed of six men selected by the officials of the member roads. Joubert, *Southern Freight Rates in Transition*, p. 34.

23. Testimony of E. D. Worcester, 43rd Congress, 1st Session (1873–74), Senate Report No. 307, Part 2, p. 127.

24. 43rd Congress, 1st Session (1873–74), Senate Report No. 307, Part 2, pp. 2–3.

25. *Ibid.*, p. 131.

26. Testimony of E. D. Worcester, 43rd Congress, 1st Session (1873–74), Senate Report No. 307, Part 2, p. 126.

27. For maps of the trunk line systems and their through freight line connections see Joseph Nimmo, Jr., *Report on the Internal Commerce of the United States . . . 1876* (Washington: Government Printing Office, 1877), maps No. 4, 5, 6 and 7. Although valuable because they are the best available, these maps are unfortunately incomplete and not always accurate in detail.

28. *Railway World*, 4:745 (August 3, 1878).

29. Boston Board of Trade, *Thirteenth Annual Report* (Boston, 1867), pp. 39–40; the Boston and Albany Railroad Company vs. the Boston and Lowell Railroad Company, 1. *Interstate Commerce Commission Reports: Decisions*, 163 (1887–1888); *Railway World*, 4:745 (August 3, 1878).

30. Testimony of G. R. Blanchard, 43rd Congress, 1st Session (1873–74), Senate Report No. 307, Part 2, p. 363.

31. 43rd Congress, 1st Session (1873–74), Senate Report No. 307, Part 2, p. 364; New York, *Proceedings of the Special Committee on Railroads. . . .* [Hepburn Committee], vol. V, p. 16 of part of volume devoted to exhibits.

32. Quoted in *Railway World*, 4:746 (August 3, 1878).

33. *American Railroad Journal*, 27:877 (August 12, 1871).

34. For a complete account of the Green Line see Joubert, *Southern Freight Rates in Transition*, pp. 31–40.

35. Testimony of Thomas E. Walker, general claim-agent, Green Line, 43rd Congress, 1st Session (1873–74), Senate Report No. 307, Part 2, p. 780.

36. 43rd Congress, 1st Session (1873–74), Senate Report No. 307, Part 1, pp. 119–120.

37. Joubert, *Southern Freight Rates in Transition*, p. 32.

38. Kirkland, *Men, Cities and Transportation*, I, 499.

39. *Ibid.*, p. 501. The secretary of the Cincinnati Chamber of Commerce stated that the first use of through bills of lading between Cincinnati and Atlantic ports occurred in 1853. Joseph Nimmo, Jr., *Report on the Internal Commerce of the United States, 1880* (Washington: Government Printing Office, 1881), Appendix, p. 234.

40. Huebner and Johnson, *The Railroad Freight Service*, p. 92.

41. 43rd Congress, 1st Session (1873–74), Senate Report No. 307, Part 1, p. 31.

42. Albert S. Bolles, *Industrial History of the United States* (Norwich, Connecticut: Henry Bill Publishing Company, 1889), p. 662.

43. David M. Ellis, "New York and the Western Trade," *New York History*, 33:388 (October, 1952).

44. *American Railroad Journal*, 33:1189 (September 22, 1877); *Railway World*, 4:745 (August 3, 1878). After a freight line had been purchased by a railroad it was operated as a freight department within the railroad company.

45. Boston Chamber of Commerce, *Sixth Annual Report* (Boston, 1891), pp. 118–119.

46. Testimony of E. D. Worcester, 43rd Congress, 1st Session (1873–74), Senate Report No. 307, Part 2, p. 127.

47. *Railway Review*, 31:57 (January 24, 1891).

48. *Ibid.*

49. Ringwalt, *Development of Transportation Systems in the United States*, p. 193.

IX. LAST STEPS IN INTEGRATION, 1880–1890

1. *American Railroad Journal*, 30:1572–1573 (December 5, 1874); and Robert J. Casey and W. A. S. Douglas, *The Lackawanna Story* (New York: McGraw-Hill, 1951), p. 94.

2. In 1880, only two short lines representing a total length of 128 miles remained.

3. *Tenth Census of the United States*, 1880, vol. IV, *Transportation*, p. 294. About 1880 the Pennsylvania, a road of 4 foot 9-inch gauge, adopted what it called a "limit gauge." Plagued by numerous tie-ups, which were caused by cars with too narrow a gauge for its tracks, the road set up rigid specifications and all cars were inspected as they came onto its line. Those that failed to fall within the specifications were rejected. There was apparently no similar "limit gauge" on any other line at this time, but in the opinion of some railroad men there should have been. *Railroad Gazette*, Fourteenth Quarto Volume (March 3, 1882), p. 133.

4. *Tenth Census of the United States*, 1880, vol. IV, *Transportation*, p. 294.

5. Edward Vernon, *American Railroad Manual for the United States and the Dominion* (New York: American Railroad Manual Company, 1873), pp. 371, 500, 501, 502.

6. Cecil Kenneth Brown, *A State Movement in Railroad Development* (Chapel Hill: The University of North Carolina Press, 1928), pp. 174–181. Throughout this study much light is thrown on the parochial viewpoint of merchant capitalism as against the unifying tendencies of finance capitalism. Another road which was changed from standard to five-foot gauge was the Montgomery and West Point in Alabama.

7. *The Merchants' Magazine*, 44:672 (June 1861), and *Tenth Census of the United States*, 1880, vol. IV, *Transportation*, p. 137.

8. From about 80 per cent to 77 per cent, if West Virginia is included with the South for both dates. Computed from *The Merchants' Magazine*, 44:672 (June 1861); *Eighth Census of the United States*, 1860, p. 331; and *Tenth Census of the United States*, 1880, vol. IV, *Transportation*, pp. 300 and 488–492.

9. *Railroad Gazette*, Thirteenth Quarto Volume (July 15, 1881), pp. 387–388.

10. *Ibid.*, Nineteenth Quarto Volume (October 14, 1887), p. 668.

11. William F. Switzler, "Report on the Internal Commerce of the United States," 49th Congress, 2nd Session (1886–87), House Executive Document No. 7, Part 2, p. 72.

12. "Of the engine builders, the Baldwin Locomotive Works had probably been the most far-seeing. For twenty years they had looked forward to this change, and had during that time so constructed their frames and fire-boxes that, by using new driving wheel centres, the change could be made without changing other parts." *Railroad Gazette*, Nineteenth Quarto Volume (November 11, 1887), p. 732.

13. The original shift was to 4 feet, 9 inches, not 4 feet, 8½ inches.

14. *Railroad Gazette*, Thirteenth Quarto Volume (July 15, 1881), pp. 387–388; Nineteenth Quarto Volume (November 11, 1887), p. 732; J. L. Ringwalt, *Development of Transportation Systems in the United States* (Philadelphia: Railway World Office, 1888), p. 358.

15. *Ibid.*

16. Charleston *News and Courier*, as quoted in Switzler, "Report on the Internal Commerce. . . ," p. 73; Kincaid A. Herr, *The Louisville & Nashville Railroad, 1850–1942* (Louisville: L. & N. Magazine, 1943), p. 47.

17. *Ibid.*, pp. 47–48; Charleston *News and Courier*, as quoted in Switzler, "Report on the Internal Commerce. . . ," pp, 72–73. A highly technical account of the problems involved in the change of gauge on the Southern roads is to be found in an article by C. H. Hudson in the *Journal of the Association of Engineering Societies*, reprinted in the *Railroad Gazette*, Nineteenth Quarto Volume (October 14, 1887), p. 668, and (November 11, 1887), pp. 731–733.

18. Herr, *Louisville & Nashville Railroad*, p. 48.

19. Charleston *News and Courier*, as quoted in Switzler, "Report on the Internal Commerce. . . ," pp. 72–73; Herr, *Louisville & Nashville Railroad*, p. 48.

20. Ringwalt, *Development of Transportation Systems in the United States*, p. 358.

21. *Ibid.* The Illinois Central, the Mobile and Ohio, and the Cincinnati, New Orleans and Texas changed to a gauge of 4 feet 8½ inches. *Railroad Gazette*, Eighteenth Quarto Volume (June 4, 1886), p. 386.

22. *Ibid.*, Nineteenth Quarto Volume (October 14, 1887), p. 668.

23. Quoted in Switzler, "Report on the Internal Commerce. . . ," p. 72.

24. *Railroad Gazette*, Nineteenth Quarto Volume (October 14, 1887), p. 668.

25. *Ibid.*, Thirty-first Quarto Volume (March 31, 1899), p. 221; *Ibid.* (September 15, 1899), pp. 644–645.

26. Herr, *Louisville & Nashville Railroad*, pp. 76–77.

Alabama

A and F	Alabama and Florida
A and MR	Alabama and Mississippi Rivers
A and TR	Alabama and Tennessee River
M and C	Marion and Cahaba
M and G	Mobile and Girard
M and WP	Montgomery and West Point

Arkansas

M and LR	Memphis and Little Rock

California

SV	Sacramento Valley

Connecticut

D and N	Danbury and Norwalk
H	Housatonic
HP and F	Hartford, Providence and Fishkill
N	Naugatuck
N and W	Norwich and Worcester
NH and N	New Haven and Northampton
NHH and S	New Haven, Hartford and Springfield
NHNL and S	New Haven, New London and Stonington
NLW and P	New London, Willimantic and Palmer
NY and NH	New York and New Haven
NYP and B	New York, Providence and Boston

Delaware

D	Delaware
DN and F	Delaware, Newcastle and Frenchtown

Florida

F	Florida
F and A	Florida and Alabama
FA and G	Florida, Atlantic and Georgia
P and G	Pensacola and Georgia
T	Tallahassee

Georgia

A and S	Augusta and Savannah
A and WP	Atlanta and West Point
B and F	Brunswick and Florida
C and S	Charleston and Savannah
CG	Central Georgia
E	Etowah
ET and G	East Tennessee and Georgia
G	Georgia
M	Muscogee
M and B	Macon and Brunswick
M and E	Milledgeville and Eatonton
M and W	Macon and Western
R	Rome
SA and G	Savannah, Albany and Gulf
SW	South Western
T and B	Thomaston and Barnesville
W and A	Western and Atlantic

Illinois

B and I	Belleville and Illinoistown
C and M	Chicago and Milwaukee
C and NW	Chicago and North Western
C and RI	Chicago and Rock Island
CB and Q	Chicago, Burlington and Quincy
G and CU	Galena and Chicago Union
GW	Great Western
IC	Illinois Central
IR	Illinois River
J and NI	Joliet and Northern Indiana
LP and B	Logansport, Peoria and Burlington
M and W	Mississippi and Wabash
P and BV	Peoria and Bureau Valley
PO and B	Peoria, Oquawka and Burlington
Q and C	Quincy and Chicago
Q and T	Quincy and Toledo
R	Rockford

Louisiana

A and C	Alexandria and Cheyneyville
BRGT and O	Baton Rouge, Grosse Tete and Opelousas
C and PH	Clinton and Port Hudson
MG	Mexican Gulf
NOO and GW	New Orleans, Opelousas and Great Western
VS and T	Vicksburg, Shreveport and Texas

Maine

A	Androscoggin
BOT and M	Bangor, Old Town and Milford
C and B	Calais and Baring
F	Franklin
GT	Grand Trunk
K and P	Kennebec and Portland
LI	Lewy's Island
P and OC	Portland and Oxford Central
PS and P	Portland, Saco and Portsmouth
S and K	Somerset and Kennebec
Y and C	York and Cumberland

Maryland

A and E	Annapolis and Elkridge
B and O	Baltimore and Ohio
C and P	Cumberland and Pennsylvania
NC	Northern Central
WM	Western Maryland

Massachusetts

AB and P	Amherst, Belchertown and Palmer
B	Berkshire
B and L	Boston and Lowell
B and M	Boston and Maine
B and P	Boston and Providence
B and W	Boston and Worcester
C	Cheshire
CC	Cape Cod
CR	Connecticut River
E	Eastern
F	Fitchburg
F and W	Fitchburg and Worcester

RI and P	Rock Island and Peoria
RI and S	Rock Island and Sterling
SLA and C	St. Louis, Alton and Chicago

Indiana

BL	Bellefontaine Line
C and C	Cincinnati and Chicago
C and M	Cincinnati and Martinsville
CP and C	Cincinnati, Peru and Chicago
E and C	Evansville and Crawfordsville
I and C	Indianapolis and Cincinnati
IC	Indiana Central
J	Jeffersonville
L and I	Lafayette and Indianapolis
LNA and C	Louisville, New Albany and Chicago
M and I	Madison and Indianapolis
MS and NI	Michigan Southern and Northern Indiana
O and M	Ohio and Mississippi
P and I	Peru and Indianapolis
SL and R	Shelbyville Lateral and Rushville
T and W	Toledo and Western
TH and R	Terre Haute and Richmond
THA and SL	Terre Haute, Alton and St. Louis

Iowa

B and M	Burlington and Missouri
CI and N	Chicago, Iowa and Nebraska
D and P	Dubuque and Pacific
DM and W	Dubuque, Marion and Western
KFDM and M	Keokuk, Fort Des Moines and Minnesota
KMP and M	Keokuk, Mt. Pleasant and Muscatine
M and M	Mississippi and Missouri

Kentucky

KC	Kentucky Central
L and BS	Lexington and Big Sandy
L and F	Louisville and Frankfort
L and N	Louisville and Nashville
NO and O	New Orleans and Ohio

FB   Fairhaven Branch
H and H   Hampshire and Hampden
MB   Marlborough Branch
N   Newburyport
NB and T   New Bedford and Taunton
NC   Norfolk County
OC and FR   Old Colony and Fall River
P and NA   Pittsfield and North Adams
P and S   Peterborough and Shirley
SB   Stony Brook
SS   South Shore
T and B   Troy and Boston
T and G   Troy and Greenfield
V and M   Vermont and Massachusetts
W   Western
W and N   Worcester and Nashua

Michigan
D and M   Detroit and Milwaukee
DM and T   Detroit, Monroe and Toledo
F and PM   Flint and Pere Marquette
GT   Grand Trunk (Toledo and Detroit branch)
MC   Michigan Central

Mississippi
GG and PG   Grand Gulf and Port Gibson
M and O   Mobile and Ohio
M and T   Mississippi and Tennessee
MC   Mississippi Central
NOJ and GN   New Orleans, Jackson and Great Northern
SM   Southern (Miss.)
WF   West Feliciana

Missouri
C and F   Cairo and Fulton
H and SJ   Hannibal and St. Joseph
NM   North Missouri
P   Pacific
PC   Platte County
Q and P   Quincy and Palmyra
SL and IM   St. Louis and Iron Mountain

New Hampshire
A   Ashuelot
BC and M   Boston, Concord and Montreal
C   Cocheco
C   Concord
C and C   Concord and Claremont
C and P   Concord and Portsmouth
CR   Contoocook River
GF and C   Great Falls and Conway
M and L   Manchester and Lawrence
N   Northern
N and L   Nashua and Lowell
WM   White Mountains

New Jersey
A   Agricultural
B and D   Belvidere and Delaware
C and A   Camden and Amboy
C and A   Camden and Atlantic
DL and W   Delaware, Lackawanna and Western
F   Flemington
H and NY   Hackensack and New York
M and E   Morris and Essex
N   Northern
N and B   Newark and Bloomfield
NJ   New Jersey
NJC   New Jersey Central
R and DB   Raritan and Delaware Bay
S   Sussex

New York
A and GW   Atlantic and Great Western
A and V   Albany and Vermont
BC and NY   Buffalo, Corning and New York
BNF and L   Buffalo, Niagara Falls and Lewiston
BNY and E   Buffalo, New York and Erie
BR and U   Black River and Utica
C   Chemung
C and S   Cayuga and Susquehanna
EJ and C   Elmira, Jefferson and Canandaigua
F and NY   Flushing and New York

H and B	Hudson and Boston
HR	Hudson River
LI	Long Island
NY and E	New York and Erie
NY and H	New York and Harlem
NYC	New York Central
O	Ogdensburgh
O and S	Oswego and Syracuse
P and M	Plattsburgh and Montreal
P and W	Potsdam and Watertown
R and LO	Rochester and Lake Ontario
R and S	Rensselaer and Saratoga
S and W	Saratoga and Whitehall
SB and NY	Syracuse, Binghamton and New York
T and G	Troy and Greenbush
W and R	Watertown and Rome

North Carolina

A and NC	Atlantic and North Carolina
NC	North Carolina
R and G	Raleigh and Gaston
RV	Roanoke Valley
W(NC)	Western (North Carolina)
W and W	Wilmington and Weldon
WC and R	Wilmington, Charlotte and Rutherford
WRNC	Western Railroad of North Carolina

Ohio

C and IJ	Cincinnati and Indianapolis Junction
C and M	Cleveland and Mahoning
C and O	Carrollton and Oneida
C and P	Cleveland and Pittsburgh
C and T	Cleveland and Toledo
C and X	Columbus and Xenia
CC and C	Cleveland, Columbus and Cincinnati
CE and R	Cincinnati, Eaton and Richmond
CH and D	Cincinnati, Hamilton and Dayton
CO	Central Ohio
CP and A	Cleveland, Painesville and Ashtabula
CP and I	Columbus, Piqua and Indiana
CW and Z	Cincinnati, Wilmington and Zanesville

CZ and C	Cleveland, Zanesville and Cincinnati
D and M	Dayton and Michigan
DX and B	Dayton, Xenia and Belpre
F and I	Fremont and Indiana
G and M	Greenville and Miami
I	Iron Railroad
LM	Little Miami
M and C	Marietta and Cincinnati
PC and C	Pittsburgh, Columbus and Cincinnati
S and C	Springfield and Columbus
S and HV	Sciota and Hocking Valley
SD and C	Sandusky, Dayton and Cincinnati
SM and N	Sandusky, Mansfield and Newark
SMV and P	Springfield, Mt. Vernon and Pittsburgh

Pennsylvania

AV	Allegheny Valley
B	Barclay
B and I	Blairsville and Indiana
B and SS	Bellefonte and Snow Shoe
BM	Beaver Meadow
C and B	Corning and Blossburg
CV	Cumberland Valley
CW and E	Catawissa, Williamsport and Elmira
D and H	Delaware and Hudson
E and P	Erie and Pittsburgh
EP	East Pennsylvania
FC	Fayette County
G	Gettysburg
H	Hempfield
H and BT	Huntingdon and Bread Top Mt.
L	Littlestown
L and B	Lackawanna and Bloomsburg
L and S	Lehigh and Susquehanna
L and T	Lockhaven and Tyrone
LSN	Little Schuylkill Navigation
LV	Lebanon Valley
LV	Lehigh Valley
LV	Lykens Valley
NP	North Pennsylvania
P	Pennsylvania

P and BC   Philadelphia and Baltimore Central
P and C   Pittsburgh and Connellsville
P and E   Philadelphia and Erie
P and R   Philadelphia and Reading
P and T   Philadelphia and Trenton
PFW and C   Pittsburgh, Fort Wayne and Chicago
PW and B   Philadelphia, Wilmington and Baltimore
Q   Quakake
S and S   Schuylkill and Susquehanna
SV and P   Shamokin Valley and Pottsville
T   Tioga
W and E   Williamsport and Elmira

Rhode Island
P and W   Providence and Worcester

South Carolina
BR   Blue Ridge
C and D   Cheraw and Darlington
C and SC   Charlotte and South Carolina
G and C   Greenville and Columbia
KM   King's Mountain
L   Laurens
NE   North Eastern
S and U   Spartanburg and Union
SC   South Carolina
W and M   Wilmington and Manchester

Tennessee
ET and G   East Tennessee and Georgia
ET and V   East Tennessee and Virginia
M and C   Memphis and Charleston
M and M   McMinnville and Manchester
M and O   Mobile and Ohio
M and O   Memphis and Ohio
MC and L   Memphis, Clarksville and Louisville
N and C   Nashville and Chattanooga
N and D   Nashville and Decatur
N and K   Nashville and Kentucky
N and N   Nashville and Northwestern
W and A   Winchester and Alabama

Texas
BBB and C   Buffalo Bayou, Brazos and Colorado
GH and H   Galveston, Houston and Henderson
H and TC   Houston and Texas Central
HT and B   Houston Tap and Brazoria
SA and MG   San Antonio and Mexican Gulf
SP   Southern Pacific
T and NO   Texas and New Orleans
WC   Washington County

Vermont
C and PR   Connecticut and Passumpsic Rivers
R and B   Rutland and Burlington
R and W   Rutland and Washington
S   Sullivan
T and B   Troy and Boston
VC   Vermont Central
WV   Western Vermont

Virginia
AL and H   Alexandria, Loudoun and Hampshire
MG   Manassas Gap
N and P   Norfolk and Petersburg
NWV   North Western of Virginia
O and A   Orange and Alexandria
P   Petersburg
P and L   Petersburg and Lynchburg (South Side)
R and D   Richmond and Danville
R and P   Richmond and Petersburg
R and YR   Richmond and York River
RF and P   Richmond, Fredericksburg and Potomac
S and R   Seaboard and Roanoke
V and T   Virginia and Tennessee
VC   Virginia Central
W and P   Winchester and Potomac

Wisconsin
B and M   Beloit and Madison
C and NW   Chicago and North Western
KR and RI   Kenosha, Rockford and Rock Island

M and C	Milwaukee and Chicago
M and H	Milwaukee and Horicon
M and M	Milwaukee and Minnesota
M and P	Milwaukee and Prairie du Chien
M and W	Milwaukee and Western
MP	Mineral Point
R and M	Racine and Mississippi
S and F	Sheboygan and Fond du Lac

Canada

B and LH	Buffalo and Lake Huron
B and O	Brockville and Ottawa
C and P	Cobourg and Peterboro
E and O	Erie and Ontario
G and C	Grenville and Carillon
GT	Grand Trunk
GW	Great Western
L and PS	London and Port Stanley
M and C	Montreal and Champlain
N	Northern
NB and C	New Brunswick and Canada
NS	Nova Scotia
O and P	Ottawa and Prescott
P and PH	Peterboro and Port Hope
PHL and B	Port Hope, Lindsay and Beavertown
Q and R	Quebec and Richmond
SJ and S	St. John and Shediac
SL and I	St. Lawrence and Industrie
SS and C	Stanstead, Shefford and Chambly
W	Welland

INDEX

INDEX

Alabama Great Southern Railroad, 80
Alabama, railroads, 42, 43, 44
Albany (N. Y.), 5, 16, 24, 71, 73
Allen, Horatio, 43
American Express Company, 69
Androscoggin and Kennebec Railroad, 20
Arkansas, railroads, 36
Atlanta (Ga.), 42, 46
Atlantic and Great Western Railroad, 54, 73
Atlantic and St. Lawrence Railroad, 18, 20
Atlantic City (N. J.), 88
Auburn and Syracuse Railroad, 24
Augusta (Me.), 20

Baltimore (Md.), 27, 29–30, 39
Baltimore and Ohio Railroad, 5, 27–28, 29, 30, 32, 33, 38, 39, 73
Bangor, Old Town and Milford Railroad, 20
Bellaire (Ohio), 33, 39
Belpre (Ohio), 33
Bills of lading, 7, 74–75, 97
Blue Line (fast freight), 63, 68, 71, 72, 73, 74
Boston (Mass.), 4, 5, 6, 15, 16, 17, 18, 50, 54–55
Boston and Lowell Railroad, 15, 69
Boston and Providence Railroad, 15
Boston and Worcester Railroad, 4, 15, 16, 50, 73
Bowling Green (Ky.), 42, 85
Bridges, 18, 22, 32, 33, 37, 40, 41, 50, 78
Brunel, Isambard Kingdom, 12
Buffalo (N. Y.), 24, 25, 30, 31, 57, 60, 71, 73
Buffalo and Erie Railroad, 68
Buffalo and Lake Huron Railway, 22
Buffalo and State Line Railroad, 31
Burkesville (Va.), 46

Cairo (Ill.), 40, 60, 79
California, railroads, 55
Camden and Amboy Railroad, 26, 28, 53
Camden and Atlantic Railroad, 88
Camden (N. J.), 28, 53
Canada, railroads, 2, 17, 20–22, 77
Car ferries, 16, 22, 29, 33, 53–54, 82

Car hoists, 60–61, 62, 63
Cars, railroad, 2, 82; changing gauge, 63, 79, "compromise gauge," 39, 59, 68; interline exchange, 26, 33, 50–51, 56, 68, 77, 81, 82–83, 98
Central of Georgia Railroad, 46
Charleston (S. C.), 5, 41–42, 43, 44
Charleston and Hamburg Railroad, 41, 43
Charleston and Savannah Railroad, 46
Chattanooga (Tenn.), 42
Chesapeake and Ohio Railroad, 78
Chicago and Elgin Railroad, 36
Chicago (Ill.), 5, 40–41, 76
Cincinnati (Ohio), 36, 39, 51, 54, 61, 78
Cincinnati, Hamilton and Dayton Railroad, 54
Cincinnati, New Orleans and Texas Railroad, 99
Cincinnati, Selma and Mobile Railroad, 80–81
Cincinnati Southern Railroad, 79, 80
City rivalries, 5, 18–20, 23, 26–30, 31, 37, 40–47, 51–52, 59
Civil War, effect, on railroads, 6, 28, 44–45, 46–47, 53–54
Clearing house, demand for, 50–51, 76
Cleveland (Ohio), 36, 39, 73
Cleveland, Columbus and Cincinnati Railroad, 73
Cleveland, Crestline and Chicago Railroad, 91
Cleveland, Painesville and Ashtabula Railroad, 31
Collingwood (Ont.), 17
Colorado, railroads, 65
Columbia (S. C.), 46
Commercial Express (fast freight line), 73
Competition, railroad, with water routes, 2–3, 4, 33–34, 56–57, 67, 74–75
Connections, interline, 16–18, 20, 24–27, 32–33, 39, 42, 46, 53–54, 59–63, 65, 68. See also names of individual railroads and cities
Consolidation, railroad, 2, 83
Continental Line (fast freight), 73–74
Corinth (Miss.), 42, 85

The University of Illinois Press
is a founding member of the
Association of American University Presses.

University of Illinois Press
1325 South Oak Street
Champaign, IL 61820-6903
www.press.uillinois.edu